Your Faith

Your Faith

A popular presentation of Catholic belief

Liguori

LIGUORI, MISSOURI

Imprimi Potest:
Richard Thibodeau, C.Ss.R.
Provincial, Denver Province
The Redemptorists

Published by Liguori Publications
Liguori, Missouri
www.liguori.org
www.catholicbooksonline.com

Nihil Obstat: Brian Ferme, PHD JCD
Censor Deputatus
Imprimatur: + Crispian Hollis
Episcopus Portus Magni October 1992

The Nihil Obstat and Imprimatur are a declaration that a book or pamphlet is considered to be free from doctrinal or moral error. It is not implied that those who have granted the Nihil Obstat and Imprimatur agree with the contents, opinions and statements expressed.

Your Faith was originally written by a team of Redemptorists of the London Province and further revised with additional material written by Rosemary Gallagher and John Trenchard, C.Ss.R. Revisions for this edition were made by Liguori Publications, Liguori, Missouri.

Interior Design: Roger Smith

Copyright © Redemptorist Publications
Revised edition 1993
U.S. revised edition copyright 2004 by Liguori Publications

Library of Congress Catalog Control Number: 2003115871

ISBN 0-7648-0998-1

Photographs: The Image Bank, Mehau Kulyk/Science Photo Library, James Stevenson/Science Photo Library, Dave toase, I Ymson, J. Brown, Robert Harding Picture Library, APA, Zefa, Metropolitan Museum of Art, Bequest of Isaac D. Fletcher, 1917. Mr. And Mrs. Issac D. Fletcher Collection. Last Supper: Rembrandt. The Supper of Emmaus 1648 (detail), Statens Museum for Kunst, Copenhagen.

Printed in the United States of America
08 07 06 05 04   5 4 3 2 1
Revised edition 2004

For through the Spirit, by faith,
we eagerly wait for the hope of righteousness.
For in Christ Jesus...the only thing that counts
is faith working through love.

Galatians 5:5–6

contents

Contents

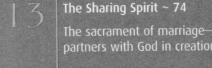

1. The Spirit of Life

From the moment we are born, life is full of surprises. There are good times, bad times, sad times, happy times. How do we make sense of this experience called life? What does it mean— this roller coaster of joy and heartbreak, hope and disillusion?

"Your whole life is changed once you have a child. I have to think about what I'm doing, where I'm going, how it will affect her. I have to plan my life now. I can no longer just drift aimlessly through my life because I have Sophie to think about and to care for."

From the moment we are born, we begin to try to make sense of life. Our struggles as a baby are signs of conflict between ourselves and the world into which we have been born.

We start life with a strong sense of self-value and self-preservation which strengthens and directs our actions and our inactions.

The way in which we develop and the kind of adults we become are determined by the way in which this instinctive self-value interacts with the circumstances and relationships we encounter.

By the time we have reached adulthood we like to think we've grown up. We've usually survived a number of painful experiences, we've made mistakes, but we've also had some good experiences. We are maturing.

But that's not the end of the story; it's only the beginning.

All through our life we will continue to ask, "What's it all about?" "What makes sense?" "What doesn't make sense?" Often it is only when we face new experiences that we are conscious that there is something more to life than we have grasped so far.

Happy experiences surprise us with unexpected pleasure, excitement, or amazement. Sad and tragic moments leave us feeling confused, lost, and asking, "There must be more to life than this?"

That magic moment of transition

"I remember walking along one day when I was about fifteen. I was at that stage in life when you yo-yo between feeling grown-up and yet still are very much part of school life. It was a hot, muggy day: A day that makes you feel summer is already here and being at school will never end. Teachers, exams, parents not understanding you, that seemed to be the total horizon of my life. Suddenly, a small toddler ran out in front of me.

"The child was laughing excitedly as his older sister chased him. Lost in the merriment, he crashed straight into me as his mother shouted, 'Watch out for that man!'

"Her words hit me ten times harder than her son. I saw myself in a new light. The monotony of the endlessness of that hot, humid day dissolved into a new image of myself as a man. I was no longer a child, somebody's son, a schoolboy. I was a man. A stranger had recognized that, had said so. It was a fleeting moment; yet now, years later, I recall it as a turning point.

"Recently, a similar incident happened again and as I heard those words, 'Watch out for that man,' all the original feelings flooded back and I relived that magic moment of transition from boy to man."

I've been pulled out of myself

"Giving birth to my little girl, Sophie, seemed to bring everything in my life into perspective. I sometimes think now that I wish I had extra time. And then I look back, before Sophie, when I had all the time in the world and I wonder what I did with it. I don't know. I didn't even seem to notice it.

"I get so much out of having her. Your whole life is changed once you have a child. I have to think about what I'm doing, where I'm going, how it will affect her. I have to plan my life now. I can no longer just drift aimlessly through my life because I have Sophie to think about and to care for. I have been pulled out of myself and forced to think beyond my own world. It's an amazing experience. As I say, everything seems to be more in perspective since I've had her."

I've worked out what matters to me

"When my partner left me for someone else I was shattered. I didn't think our relationship was perfect but we had been through a number of ups and downs, survived and, I thought, grown closer as a result. I couldn't believe that this was the end. Yet I wasn't sure whether I could rebuild something that had been so deliberately smashed by someone I had trusted.

"I felt rejected, humiliated and—later—angry, very angry. It was the usual story, everyone else seemed to know about the affair before me. Our children were confused, they asked questions I couldn't answer, they needed support, reassurance, and patient handling. The problem was, I needed these things too, so it was difficult for all of us. We limped along for many months. The only news we heard from their father seemed to be that he had made the right decision. Great for him! It didn't help us at all.

"Eventually, I started to pick up the pieces. I began to look at myself, my life, the children's future, and who and what we had become. I was forced to reassess almost every part of my existence and, looking back, it was a good exercise. Before he left, we were chugging along in a happy cocoon. Life ran through my fingers like dry sand from the beach. Now I value everything so much more; I've worked out what matters to me."

A restlessness had stirred in me

"I don't know what caused my breakdown really. It wasn't a single event or crisis. In fact, I was walking through the park on my way to work last spring, when a feeling of utter desolation swept over me. I was surrounded by signs of new life: bulbs in flower, the birds chattering, and my heart felt like lead.

"I have a successful career, enough money, a pleasant home, and a wife and family who give me security and a sense of belonging. And yet my life seems strangely empty and meaningless.

"The feeling of isolation and being adrift on a sea of nothingness is powerful and all-pervading. Throughout the summer that followed, those feelings of dissatisfaction and almost a desperate kind of loneliness seeped into my days. My wife showed kindly concern and put it down to the mid-life crisis. She assured me it would pass.

"But a restlessness had stirred in me. Material possessions and human achievement are somehow not enough anymore. I have begun to read more and listen to other people as they talk about their philosophy or way of life. I am conscious of searching for something to complete my incompleteness. I know there must be more meaning to life than what I have experienced. I think recognizing that is an important step for me."

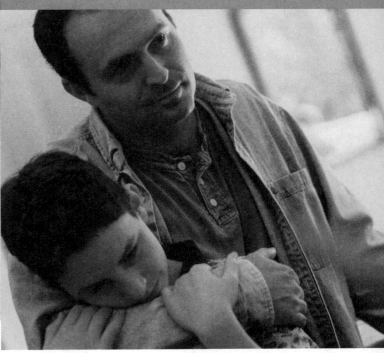

I didn't think I would be able to get through it

"Lots of people in my school come from divorced families but I didn't know it at the time my parents split up. My Mom and Dad used to fight a lot and I was very afraid that they would separate. I didn't think I would be able to get through it but now that I've experienced it I know you can if you persevere.

"When my Dad walked out, I was worried that my Mom would leave as well. I thought it was my fault that he went in the end. My sister and I had been fighting and he was angry. I thought I wouldn't see him again.

"We didn't know what was happening for about two days. He just went and my Mom didn't say anything; then she told us. I felt all churned up inside as though no one cared what was happening to me and my sister. I kept hoping he would come back, that things would be the same as before and we would be a typical family. I got so that I didn't want to talk to anyone. I used to fight with my sister and break her things. I felt cut off, I thought everyone else had a Dad except me.

"Now my Dad has got a new wife and we see him about three or four times a year. I've got used to it now. We've moved three times and that's hard—new friends, new school, new home. Some friends are helpful, others are not; they just spread what you tell them around the school. If you don't have anyone to talk to, you just have to try to trust someone. I get very sad sometimes when I've seen my Dad and we have to go home. I don't know if I want to get married because I think the same thing is going to happen to me and it frightens me."

I love you

"The words are commonplace; yet, to me, they meant very little. I wanted sex (who doesn't?) but I also wanted non-involvement and my independence. These are the principles that I was taught even as a child. As it became clearer that she loved me, I remember that my reaction was to run away. I told her not to nag me and to leave me alone. Then, when she left me alone (she was used to dealing with children) I reacted angrily.

"One cold winter evening, I was lost more than usual in frustration and tears. I remember saying, 'If I tell you I love you that means more than I can give you.' I wanted to escape but she held me in her arms. It must have been her warmth that took me out of myself and enabled me to say, 'I love you.' "

I feel I've given him his life back

"When my second son, Alan, was born, the doctors at the hospital told me that he was suffering from a dysplastic kidney condition that prevented his kidney from growing. We waited for over two years for a donor but without success. I couldn't face the thought of my little boy growing up year after year with uncertainty and dialysis treatment every day. I decided to ask the doctors if I would be a suitable donor. Alan and I had our operations on the same day and the whole thing has been a great success. I feel I've given him his life back.

"Life's difficult but it's still worth living. At least now Alan's got a chance. I'm only an ordinary working man but I feel overwhelmed that I could give my child such a gift. I don't really know what to make of it."

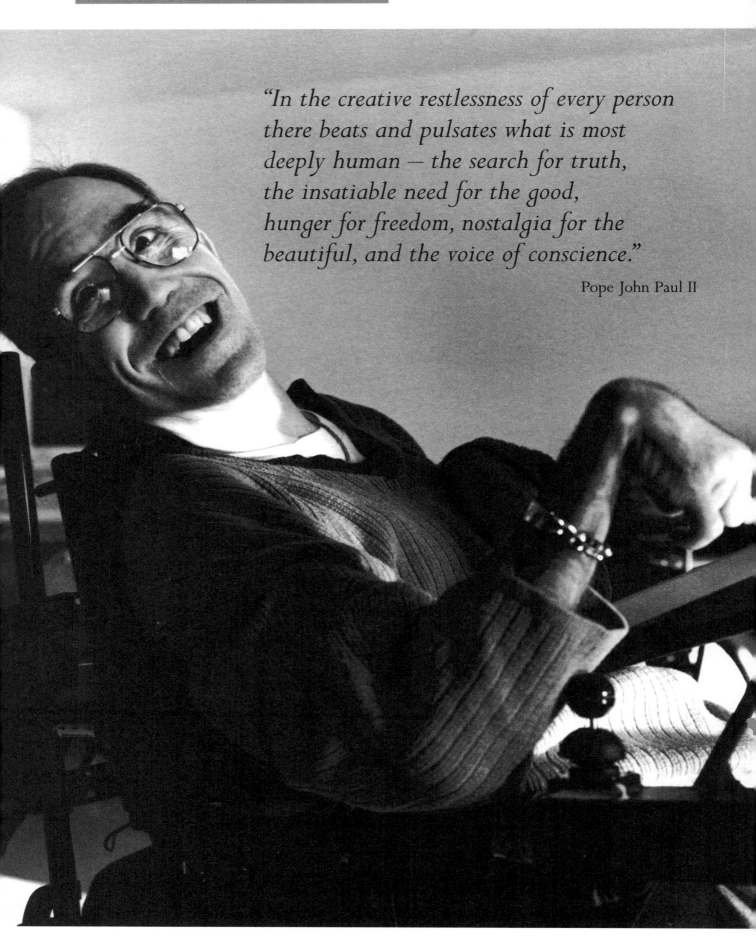

"In the creative restlessness of every person there beats and pulsates what is most deeply human — the search for truth, the insatiable need for the good, hunger for freedom, nostalgia for the beautiful, and the voice of conscience."

Pope John Paul II

Change never leaves us as it finds us

As we journey through life, we face continual change and from time to time sudden change occurs which stops us in our tracks. Our personal map for living life which we had worked out so well is somehow no longer applicable. It doesn't fit our new and changed experience and we have to redraw our map for life once again.

At the heart of all this tension, change, and complexity of life remain those fundamental questions, "What is life all about, where am I going, what does it all mean?" And the root of these questions takes us back to our first days of life when we were at the center of our tiny world; a time before we had been forced to adapt and adjust to the world and the people around us. That sense of total self-worth is the most important treasure we possess. And as we look at the kind of changes that all people experience, we can learn to extend ourselves into an even more complete wholeness of being, unique, precious, and of irreplaceable value. This is a wholeness built not on isolation or power but through the extension and completion of the potential we had as a newly born person.

It is a paradox that we can only reach that full potential of ourselves through our interaction with others and through a willingness to, and an acceptance of, change as part of life. Facing change can always help us to grow.

Yet we fear change; we are afraid of things never being the same, afraid of the unknown, afraid that change will demolish us. And so we avoid change as much as possible. We tend to refuse to face new changes in our lives and in our bodies because we want to cling to what is familiar, what is known. In one sense, we are like an unborn child still within the womb. Such a child is safe, warm, protected from the outside world. But such a child is also growing, developing, maturing. There comes a time when the womb can no longer contain the child or supply all that is needed for continued growth and development. Birth is imminent; a major life change, from all that is familiar, safe, tried, and tested, into unknown territory with only our potential to bring with us.

Each of us has been through that major life change of birth into a totally new world. And every change we have negotiated since will have been a mini-birth in terms of new experience and growth. Only when we have resisted or refused change have we stopped growing, stopped learning, and begun to kill off our potential for life.

What is this life force, then, which pulls us on, often in spite of our resistance and reluctance? Why do we experience a restlessness and dissatisfaction with life even when we have ample material goods? Where does that powerful magnet we call love come from, the kind of love that makes us feel brand new again, full of life, enthusiastic and whole?

The starting point of our Christian faith is our own human experience. If you look back on your own life, you will recall experiences that were successful and happy but also you will remember experiences that were painful and which stretched you to the limit. Looking back on such experiences forces us to look forward and to recognize that there seems to be no limit to the human spirit. This is equally true of the life of the human race.

It is our Christian faith that tells us that every single person is touched by God and that the experiences that draw us to a deeper sense of our self-value and the greatness of the human spirit are the work of God within us.

The experience of people throughout the ages has led them to believe that there is something more to life than simply what they see and understand from their senses. For a large number, the answer has been a belief system, a religion. But many people will say that religion doesn't provide the answers. In fact, in their search for meaning in life, they often reject religion as hypocritical, a power structure, or a myth which pacifies and tranquilizes those who cannot face the fundamental truths of life.

Such a reaction is a wholly sound one on which to base any search for the meaning of life because it is founded upon a search for truth and authenticity. It is a search for something which makes sense of human experience and which will not be deceived by second-hand answers dealt out by others rather than answers which ring true to a personal experience of life.

Dr. M. Scott Peck in his book, *The Road Less Traveled*, poses the question which must be at the heart of any serious attempt to understand the meaning of life and the meaning of a religious response to our questioning. He asks whether the question is really "What has God done to humans?" or should it rather be "What have humans done to God?"

All too often human beings, in talking about God or explaining the meaning of their religion, teach us more about human nature than about the nature of God. When we look at the history of peoples' religious quest, we see it overlaid with human characteristics which have often distorted or muddied any images or experiences of God. And yet the rumor of the Spirit of God remains as strong as ever in the hearts and lives of men and women. Even those who claim to have no belief in a God will often admit to praying in times of serious need or loss.

The spiritual dimension within each one of us is a call to something beyond ourselves. It is a hunger of the heart; a longing for something more, a relationship which will complete us and fulfill our unspoken needs. True religion is not the imposition of sets of rules; it is the discovery of a relationship which helps us make sense of life and leads us to the fullness of life.

Throughout history, men and women have tried hard to find meaning in their existence and their experiences. We have always asked the questions: What is the meaning and purpose of life? What is upright behavior and what is sinful? Where does suffering originate and why do we suffer? How can genuine happiness be found? What happens at death? What is the ultimate mystery from which we take our origin and towards which we tend? The developments in the universal search for meaning can be seen in the diversity of world religions:

2. The Rumor of the

Islam is closely linked to the Christian and Jewish faiths in that its basis is to be found in the Old Testament. The name "Islam" means submission (to God), and that is the path Muslims are called to follow. They worship God, who is one, almighty, and merciful. They strive to submit to God's plan and, in this, they follow Abraham. They do not, however, acknowledge Jesus Christ as God, although they venerate him as a prophet and honor Mary, his virgin Mother. They follow the teaching of the prophet Muhammad (who lived about AD 600) and who, they believe, gives them the final revelation of the true path to God.

Buddhism is a very long-established religious tradition which dates back to the sixth century BC. It is a way of life which centers on the teaching of the Buddha who leads his followers on a path to enlightenment based on the four Noble Truths: the fact of pain or evil; that pain has a cause; that pain can be ended; and that it can be ended by following the Eightfold Way—of right views, right intention, right speech, right action, right livelihood, right effort, right mindfulness, and right concentration. This form of enlightenment testifies to the essential inadequacy of a changing world and to the possibility of reaching supreme illumination.

Hinduism is really a comprehensive group of many beliefs and practices all of which center on the worship of different gods and on guidance by gurus. Hinduism varies enormously, from place to place, and there is a wide range of structures, festivals, and caste systems associated with it. As with Buddhism, the ultimate goal of Hinduism is deliverance from the cycle of continual birth and death. Release is sought from the trials of the present life by ascetical practices, profound meditation, and recourse to God in confidence and love.

As Christians we respect the many rich insights, the manner of life, and the teachings of other religions, recognizing their significant contribution to the search for truth. The Christian Church, however, has a particular closeness to the religion known as

Judaism, which provides the foundation of faith for followers of Jesus Christ. The beginnings of Christian belief are to be found in the faith and election by the one, true God of Abraham, the patriarchs, Moses, and the prophets. This revelation of himself by God, which called into being the Jewish people, is recorded in the book known to the Jews as the Torah and, to Christians, as the first five books of the Old Testament....

The developments in the universal search for meaning can be seen in the diversity of world religions.

Spirit of God

The Old Testament

Our human experience and our search for meaning is recorded in a unique way in what Christians call the "Old Testament." It is unique for two reasons:

- First, it records the struggle of a people—the Jewish people—to make sense of life and, in particular, to enter into a relationship with God.

- Second, and much more important, it records the efforts of God to enter into a relationship with his chosen people.

Let's look at both of these statements

First, the Jewish people were unique in their growing realization that there is only one God. Other peoples worshiped the gods of nature or the gods of their ancestors. In the thousand years prior to the birth of Jesus Christ, the Jews came to recognize that there is only one God, the creator of the universe, who was intimately involved in their happiness and success. This was not an easy process. There were times in Jewish history when they were exiled from their own country and suffered the most dreadful agonies and humiliations yet, as time went on, they grew in their understanding of God's love.

Second (and again, much more important), God is recognized in the Old Testament as taking the initiative in letting himself be known to his people. And God is not seen in the Old Testament as remote or uncaring but, rather, as "moved by compassion" to care for his people. So startling is this "revelation"—a truth that could never be conceived of by human effort—that the Old Testament is described as the "Word of God."

Perhaps one of the closest human parallels to the relationship between God and the Jewish people is the love between parent and child. This relationship is one of total dependency but not without its difficult moments and tensions. There are frustrations on both sides as parent and child struggle towards mutual understanding and intimacy. In the Jewish people of the Old Testament, we see the effort to be "grown up," to "make a name for themselves," to be like God; and in the God of the Old Testament we see the frustration of every parent to make their love known to their child—it is the Lord who "will wipe away the tears from every cheek" and who is "like someone who lifts an infant close against his cheek, stooping down to him to give him his food."

For most people today, the Old Testament is not an "easy read." This is not because its message lacks excitement or because the stories are lackluster. On the contrary! Yet some guidance is helpful in reading the Old Testament, which comes to us not as a single book but as a collection of over forty books and writings assembled over the period of nearly a thousand years. It is a "library," much of which we would dip into rather than attempt to read at a single sitting. For the follower of Jesus Christ, however, the Old Testament is essential reading. It is necessary for the following reasons:

- The Old Testament reveals a wholly unique relationship between the one God and a specially chosen people. The God who is revealed and worshiped by the Jews is the One whom Jesus was to call his "Father."

- The Old Testament asks the questions and tackles the issues that confront every human being. The Jews faced the very difficult questions. The answers to those questions were the result of much searching and only finally realized in the life and work of Jesus Christ.

- The world of the Old Testament was the world into which Jesus Christ was born. Even as a young boy he was taught the essentials of the story of his people. As he began his studies Jesus was given a slate with passages of Scripture (the Old Testament) written on it. The slate was also smeared with honey—a sign of the teaching he was to absorb. In his sufferings, Jesus reflected the life of the Jewish people of the Old Testament. Many of his teachings were taken directly from the Old Testament.

The Old Testament, then, "foreshadows" the life of Jesus Christ. It gives an outline or shape of what is to come in Jesus Christ. The Old Testament provides us with an outline picture of God. And Jesus Christ throws light on this picture so that the face of God is fully revealed. As Saint Augustine of Hippo was to write: "In the Old Testament the New is hidden; in the New Testament the Old is laid open."

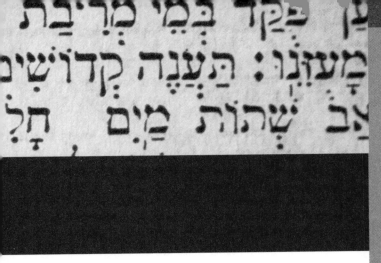

עֵן אֶפְקֹד בְּמֵי מְרִיבַת
מֵעֻזֵּנוּ: תַּעֲנֶה קְדוֹשִׁים
אָב שָׁרוֹת מַיִם חָל

The most important texts of the Old Testament

The most important texts of the Old Testament are its first five books which make up the Torah or Pentateuch. The Pentateuch outlines

■ How God "chose" Israel to be his own people, beginning with his promise to Abraham to make him the "father of a multitude of nations...and his descendants as many as the stars of heaven" (Genesis 17:5; 22:17).

■ How God made a "covenant" or "contract" with the Jews to make them the channel of his mercy if they kept the laws he gave them. And so to Moses, the dominant figure of the Pentateuch and the whole Old Testament, God says, "I will adopt you as my own people, and I will be your God" (Exodus 6:7).

■ How God gave the law to Israel as the most direct revelation of his will. This law is symbolized in the tradition that the Ten Commandments were originally inscribed by God on two tablets of stone: The Lord said, "I am the Lord your God, who rescued you from Egypt where you were slaves."

1. Worship no god but me. Do not make for yourselves images of anything in heaven or on earth or in the water under the earth. Do not bow down to any idol or worship it, for I am the Lord your God and I tolerate no rivals.
2. Do not use my name for evil purposes for I, the Lord your God, will punish anyone who misuses my name.
3. Observe the Sabbath and keep it holy, as I, the Lord your God have commanded you.
4. Respect your father and your mother.
5. Do not commit murder.
6. Do not commit adultery.
7. Do not steal.
8. Do not accuse anyone falsely.
9. Do not desire another man's wife.
10. Do not desire his house, his land, his slaves, his cattle, his donkeys or anything else he owns (Deuteronomy 5:6-21).

The Rumor of the Spirit of God

The principal names of God's chosen people used in the Old Testament

HEBREW: This term originally meant "nomad," literally, "one from across the river" (a reference to the exodus of God's people from Egypt). It is the name usually given to the Jews of earlier times and also to the language.

JEW: This term is derived from "Judah" (a son of Jacob) and a tribe descended from him. The Kingdom of Judah became the nucleus of the Jewish people.

ISRAEL: This name is one given to the Jewish people, originally to Jacob as the ancestor of the people of God: "Your name shall no longer be Jacob, but Israel" (Genesis 32:28). Israel means "God struggles" or "God is strong."

The Names of God

There are two principal names for God in the Old Testament.

YAHWEH: A personal form of the name of God that appears more than 6,000 times in the Old Testament. This name is thought to be a form of a verb meaning "to be" and has a connotative meaning of "one who causes existence." Yahweh of the Old Testament is the God of the covenant, one who creates, maintains, and sustains the natural world.

ELOHIM: Another divine name frequently used in the Hebrew text of the Old Testament and a plural form of Eloah. When this term is used of the God of Israel, it signifies the one God who possesses in himself all the qualities of divinity. When Elohim is used for the true God, its modifiers and accompanying verbs are almost always in the singular. Examples of this use are found in Psalm 7:10, "righteous God"; 2 Kings 19:4, "living God"; and Genesis 48:21, "God be with you." Genesis 2:4 in the Hebrew text gives an example of the use of Elohim and Yahweh as identical in meaning, as in the following passage from Exodus 3:14: "And God (Elohim) said to Moses, 'I Am who I Am (Yahweh).' "

The moment when God revealed his name to Moses comes in one of the most significant passages in the Bible: "Then Moses said to God, 'I am to go, then, to the sons of Israel and say to them, "The God of your fathers has sent me to you." But if they ask me what his name is, what am I to tell them?' And God said to Moses, 'I Am who I Am. This,' he added, 'is what you must say to the sons of Israel: "I Am has sent me to you." ' And God also said to Moses, 'You are to say to the sons of Israel: "Yahweh, the God of your fathers, the God of Abraham, the God of Isaac, and the God of Jacob, has sent me to you." This is my name for all time; by this name I shall be invoked for all generations to come'" (Exodus 3:13-15).

Is the Old

Jesus Christ did not burst in on a world wholly unprepared for him.

Looking back we can recognize in the Old Testament how God was preparing a way for the coming of Jesus Christ. And if we look back to the Old Testament and try to pinpoint the single most important event in the history of the Jewish people we would have to say that everything surrounding the "Exodus" from slavery in Egypt was such an event. However, to isolate this moment in such a way would be misleading. It was more their prayerful reflection and deepening understanding of the meaning of this event than the event itself that formed the Jewish people in their special relationship with God.

It is important, then, to understand what kind of history the Old Testament presents. Usually, the Old Testament is divided into three kinds of books—History, Poetry (or Wisdom), and Prophecy. But all the writings—even the History—are concerned with the relationship between the Jews and God.

The history found in the Old Testament is not written in the clinical fashion of the modern historian. When, for example, Bishop James Ussher in 1654 used the "information" in the Bible to calculate the creation of the world at 4004 BC, he was totally misunderstanding the Old Testament. The Bible has one purpose and one alone: it tells of the deepening relationship between God and men and women—the single most significant fact of history since creation itself. The Bible is a history of "salvation."

Understanding the meaning of the writing

The Church assures us that "the books of Scripture must be acknowledged as teaching firmly, faithfully, and without error that truth which God wanted put into the sacred writings for the sake of our salvation" (Vatican II). It is the word of God, but "God speaks in sacred Scripture through men in human fashion." Even when provided with a good translation (and no translation can ever be quite like the original), we still have the task of unraveling the meaning of what has been written.

It is obvious that unless we understand the kind of writing that appears in the Old Testament we can make some very silly mistakes. We can totally misread the word of God; just as a second-century Roman citizen could completely fail to grasp what our society was like in 2003 through misreading the daily newspapers.

The Old Testament is not really about history or geography — it's about salvation

There is one, vital fact about the Old Testament which we must always have at the front of our minds. The word of God is concerned with salvation. It is not concerned with history or geography or any form of science. It is concerned with our salvation. It draws to our attention the relationship which exists between God and men and women.

And to understand what God is saying about our salvation, we have to pay serious attention to the customary way in which people of the time thought and expressed themselves. We must also bear in mind the customs of the day and the way in which people related to one another and dealt with one another in their day-to-day existence at the time of writing.

The Books of the Old Testament

The Old Testament records the struggle of the Jewish people to make sense of life and to enter into a relationship with God. It also records God's relationship with his world and his people.

In conveying this development, the Old Testament has been called a library of books, and the three main sections of this library are as follows:

History and Law

These books record both the historical story of the Jewish people and also the story of the gift of the Covenant, or Law, which God gave them. The story of the ways in which they kept or failed to keep the Law is threaded through their years of recorded history.

- **The early years:** Genesis, Exodus, Leviticus, Numbers, Deuteronomy.
- **Their settlement and exile:** Joshua, Judges, Ruth, 1 and 2 Samuel, 1 and 2 Kings, 1 and 2 Chronicles.

- **Release from captivity to resettlement:** Ezra, Nehemiah, Tobit, Judith, Esther, 1 and 2 Maccabees.

Wisdom

These books record the customs, worship, and understanding of the great thinkers of the Jewish people. In these books we can discover their philosophy of life, their poetry, and their understanding of their special relationship with God: Job, Psalms, Proverbs, Ecclesiastes, Song of Solomon, Wisdom, Ecclesiasticus (Sirach).

Prophets

While containing a considerable amount of historical information, these books are principally focused upon the teachings and preaching of the prophets, the wise men of the Jewish people through the ages: Isaiah, Jeremiah, Lamentations, Baruch, Ezekiel, Daniel, Hosea, Joel, Amos, Obadiah, Jonah, Micah, Nahum, Habakkuk, Zephaniah, Haggai, Zechariah, Malachi.

Testament History?

How do Christians deepen their understanding of the Old Testament?

The one, true God originally revealed himself over many centuries to a people whose origins are to be found in the lives of Abraham, Isaac, and Jacob (about 1800 BC), and continuing to the birth of Jesus Christ. During this period the Old Testament was mostly written in Hebrew—the language of the Jewish people. In this way, the word of God was expressed at a particular time in history and in human words.

At the time of Jesus Christ few could speak the Hebrew language and so it was translated into Aramaic and Greek. Since then, and helped by the spread of the Christian Church, the Old Testament in its entirety has been translated into 262 languages.

If we are to deepen our understanding of God's word, then, we must understand exactly **what** was written, we must understand **when** it was written, and we must understand **why** it was written.

And so to understand what God is saying to us today through the Old Testament we have to answer two questions:

- What does the text actually say?
- What did it mean to the Jewish people at the time?

Read the five pieces of text on the right carefully. They are all taken from newspapers published on one day. "Invaders from Mars" won't mean much to you unless you saw the film, nor will the reference to the bar code at Morriston Hospital unless you are a regular supermarket shopper. The book review is clear enough if you are familiar with the workings of the CIA. When we learn that the clip about the husband being persuaded to jump off his broomstick is from a gossip column, we will probably take it with a grain of salt. The meaning of the horoscope depends on your view of such things.

We can well imagine the confusion in the mind of a native of Palestine about 100 BC if he or she was faced with these newspaper extracts. Even if provided with a good translation (and how do you translate words like "bar code," "computerized," into good second-century Hebrew?) the meaning of the texts is not self-evident. What is a "brain-drain"? Do the inhabitants of this country really direct their lives according to the stars?

Article 1: Book Review

non-fiction
Joseph Losey
The account of the life of film director Joseph Losey represents the other side of the CIA coin, for Losely was forced into exile after the House Un-American Activities Committee labeled him a Communist.

Article 2: Horoscope

Aquarius
Jan 23 to Feb 19
The sun is in Scorpio now. Matters of career or professional nature come into sharp focus and somewhere along the line you must be prepared to go against the tide of opinion and do what you should have done months ago.

Article 3: Advice Column

I would gladly pay their airfare myself and, in extreme cases, be quite happy to rustle up unmarried female relatives of my American husband who might be persuaded to jump the broomstick if a Green Card were in the offing. Whatever, just go, will you? Remember the Brain Drain in the Seventies? We could call this the Pain Drain.

Article 4: TV Guide Entry

6:00 p.m.: "Invaders from Mars" Director William Cameron creates a '50s fantasy favorite about a small-town American boy (Jeremy Hart) who sees a flying saucer land but nobody believes him. It explores the paranoid 1950s territory of "aliens gone mad," best exemplified by the 1956 masterpiece *Invasion of the Body Snatchers*.

Artice 5: News Article

In a pioneering plan at Morriston Hospital, patients are being issued their own unique bar code rather like a can of baked beans in a supermarket. But the only cart they are likely to come near is the one used on the drug rounds.

The bar code is strapped to the patient's wrist and acts as a form of identification. So nurses only need to scan the code, like a clerk in a shop, to obtain details of the patient's prescription on the screen of an accompanying computer. The patient's bar code is cross referenced with the one input by the doctor at the time of prescribing and with the one on the bottle of drugs in the drug cabinet.

The Psalms

The psalms are prayers of people who regarded God as a friend. There was no need to hide their true feelings when they were in his presence. And so when they prayed, they complained, they questioned, they cajoled. At first sight, some of the things they said to God surprise us. We have a way of wanting to be on our best behavior when we pray and keep a respectful attitude. This was not the approach taken by the psalms. If things were bad, then there was no point in glossing over the badness in order to impress God. There was no misfortune or misery which God would not understand.

So they meant what they said when they talked about being wronged, hurt, even rejected. God was not above and beyond all this. It was his world and he held the reins. The famous Psalm 22, which was prayed by Jesus on the cross, is a good illustration of this:

My God, my God, why have you forsaken me?
You are far from my plea and the cry of my distress.
O my God, I call by day and you give no reply;
I call by night and I find no peace (Psalm 22:1-2).

If the prayer had ended there or simply continued in that vein, then it might have been open to the criticism that it was indulging in self-pity or bitterness. But it did not end there. After the prayers of the Psalms had said how badly they felt, they were able to step outside of themselves and look to God. There followed invariably a protestation of confidence in the Almighty. Contrary to appearances, he had not left them. He could never abandon them. His help was sure to come. Nothing was more certain than that.

Yet you, O God, are holy,
enthroned on the praises of Israel.
In you our fathers put their trust;
they trusted and you set them free.
When they cried to you, they escaped.
In you they trusted and never in vain (Psalm 22:3-5).

With this renewed trust in God they went on to make their petitions. This they did in a restrained way. Their requests were made in general terms. There was no need to suggest to God what he might do. They were sure that he would do something and they could safely leave to his wisdom the choice of what was to be done.

It is interesting to see that in these psalms a process is going on which soothes the human spirit. People who start off their prayer with their spirits at a low ebb work through to a trust in God which results in a restrained but confident plea for God's continuing protection.

O Lord, do not leave me alone, my strength, make haste to help me! Rescue my soul from the sword (Psalm 22:19-20).

3. The Spirit of the Lord has been given to me

A Messiah on the horizon

The Old Testament records God's relationship with his people and the ways in which he communicated his message to them through their experiences and through their prophets. At the heart of this relationship was the promise and the growing confidence that a Messiah would come. God would send his people a new leader, a king, a guide to freedom, peace, and fulfillment. A Messiah was on the horizon for the People of God.

The Christ, the Messiah and the Jews

The people of Nazareth would have been amazed to know that some people nowadays think that "Christ" is the surname of Jesus. For them the Christ, whom they called in their own language the Messiah, was the hope of Israel. He would come and restore the glory which their most beloved king, David, had brought to Israel. Not only would he restore their lost glory but he would make them the greatest nation on earth.

The great questions in the synagogues were about the Messiah. When would he come? What would he be like?

In Jesus' time, and particularly when he lived in Galilee, there was a great deal of disagreement about the answer to these questions. One Galilean group called the Zealots believed that the coming of Christ was imminent and, to prepare the country for his coming, they resorted to guerrilla tactics to overthrow the foreign government of Rome. Another group, the Essenes, who lived in a sort of community at Qumran, near the Dead Sea, believed that two messiahs would come; one would be their priest, the other would be their king.

All the Jews believed that it was essential to prepare for the coming of the Messiah. They didn't necessarily agree, however, on how they should prepare. A group called the Pharisees followed a very strict way of life which kept them apart from all foreigners. They felt it was necessary for the Jews to be a "people apart" for only then would they understand the message the Messiah would preach.

Although the Jews had different ideas about the sort of person the Messiah would be, they eagerly looked forward to his coming. The followers of Jesus had grown up against this background of expectancy. They, like everyone else, looked forward to the coming of the Messiah.

In any event, many rejected Jesus because he didn't fit in with their ideas of what the Messiah should be like.

Looking back, it's easy for us to see that the coming of Jesus Christ was indeed a turning point in the history of men and women. A new era did begin in Nazareth all those years ago. But it was not the era expected by the reformers, the Zealots, the establishment, or the scholars of the time. It was something that perhaps most people had never dared hope for. From that day when Jesus unrolled the scroll in the synagogue at Nazareth the world would never be the same again: because Jesus proclaimed the coming of a kingdom totally beyond all human expectations.

As we know from our own experiences it is often only after an event, when we look back on it, that we see its true significance and its effect upon us. Only on reflection do we understand what has happenend to us. It was the same with men's and women's experience and understanding of Jesus Christ in his own time. They listened to him, they saw miraculous signs but only gradually, as the years went by, did they really begin to grasp the full significance of his words, his actions, and his life.

The final prophet

The last prophet in the history of God's relationship with men and women pointed to the presence of the Lord, the Messiah in their midst. John the Baptist was a Jew, he had no fixed home but moved around Judaea and the banks of the river Jordan calling on people to change their ways, to claim their true freedom, and to turn back wholeheartedly to God. He baptized people in the river water as a sign of their change of heart and their readiness to be open to the Spirit of God speaking in their hearts.

John the Baptist was the man that the prophet Isaiah spoke of when he wrote hundreds of years earlier:

> **A voice cries in the wilderness:**
> **Prepare a way for the Lord,**
> **make his paths straight (Isaiah 40:3).**

John was known to be a very good, a very sincere man. Even Jewish historians of the time recorded this fact. It was not surprising, then, that some people began to think that John was the much-longed-for Messiah. For an oppressed people, as the Jews were at that time, a new king bringing freedom and liberation seemed to be the answer to their prayers. But John was quick to point out to his many followers that he was simply the forerunner, the link between the laws of the Old Testament and a new era. Men and women were to be born again in God's Spirit in order to become fully united with their Creator and the source of all real love.

John baptizes Jesus

One day, when John was baptizing people in the river Jordan, a man called Jesus of Nazareth appeared through the crowd and asked for baptism. John's reaction is significant; he tried to dissuade Jesus, claiming that it was Jesus who should baptize him. But Jesus insisted, and Jesus' baptism by John became the sign that the preparation for the coming of the Messiah was over. Jesus of Nazareth is the Messiah; the Spirit of God is seen to be with him, and the new age which will fulfill and perfect the old one has begun.

After his baptism, Jesus came to Nazareth, where he had been brought up, and went into the synagogue on the sabbath day as he usually did. He stood up to read, and the scroll of the prophet Isaiah was handed to him. Unrolling the scroll he found the place where it is written:

> **The spirit of the Lord has been given to me,**
> **for he has anointed me.**
> **He has sent me to bring the good news to the poor,**
> **to proclaim liberty to captives**
> **and to the blind new sight,**
> **to set the downtrodden free,**
> **to proclaim the Lord's year of favor (Luke 4:18-19).**

He then rolled up the scroll, gave it back to the assistant and sat down. And all eyes in the synagogue were fixed on him. Then he began to speak to them, "This text is being fulfilled today even as you listen" (Luke 4:21).

These words were the starting point of the life work of Jesus. And immediately they presented a challenge to those who heard him. Some were "astonished by the gracious words that came from his lips." Others doubted his credentials and tried to kill him. This is a recurring pattern of reaction throughout the life of Jesus. There is constant tension between those who can accept his words and those who find him unbelievable.

Who Is JESUS CHRIST?

march 2003

Four days dead

Yesterday in the little village of Bethany two miles from Jerusalem, a man was brought back to life after lying in the grave for four days.

Witnesses at the scene claim they saw the rabbi Jesus approach the grave and order the stone to be removed...

Two thousand years ago there were no newspapers and so the above report could only have been spread by word of mouth. Nonetheless, we might expect that if the marvelous words and deeds recorded in the Gospels are genuine, the exciting news they contain would have exploded throughout the known world. And yet the truth is that Jesus Christ is barely mentioned outside the Gospels. Critics of our faith are quick to seize on this, "If Jesus did all that you claim," they object, "why was his life so little known and why did it end in such humiliation? Surely, an impartial observer must have written something about this extraordinary man?"

How, then, did Jesus appear to those who lived with him? If we travel back in time and ask one of them, "Who is Jesus?" we might get the following information.

Jesus grew up in a town called Nazareth in the central region of Galilee. The little town was home to about five hundred people, some of whom were not of Jewish descent. Trade routes and roads passed near Nazareth, but the village itself, mainly agricultural, was not on any main road.

The people in Jerusalem, about ninety miles to the south, did not have much time for the Nazarenes. They thought that they mixed rather too much with foreigners and spoke with a rough, vulgar accent.

Nazareth was the sort of place you made jokes about, and Nazarenes were the sort of people you jeered at. So when Nathaniel, a man who later became one of Jesus' followers, first heard about Jesus, he laughingly asked, "Can anything good come out of Nazareth?"

Jesus began his life as a village carpenter. At first he seemed to do quite well for himself. He became a "rabbi"—a teacher of the Scriptures. Gradually, his reputation spread, and he began to be accepted as a man who was successfully trying to purify the old Jewish religion.

But then he went too far. Priests and people knew that reforms were needed, but when they realized that this man was demanding more than the alteration of a few laws, they became angry. Eventually, because he claimed to be God, they had him crucified.

Those are the facts. There doesn't seem much to write about. Unless, of course, the writer believed that Jesus really was God. The writers who did believe this wrote down his life in the Gospels.

It should be clear that if we went back to ask someone who knew him, "Who is Jesus?" the reply would have been more than a few facts. We would probably get one of the following statements:

1. "They hanged Jesus of Nazareth on the eve of the Passover because he practiced sorcery and was leading Israel astray."
2. "You can all be certain that God has made this Jesus whom you crucified both Lord and Christ."

Which of these statements do you agree with? The first is by a Jewish historian who lived at the same time as Christ, the second is by Saint Peter on the day of Pentecost. You obviously cannot agree with both statements because they contradict each other. But you have to agree with one of them.

Clearly, there can be no such thing as an "impartial observer" of Christ's life. We *have* to make a choice. As Jesus tells us, "He who is not with me is against me" (Matthew 12:30).

He was born in an obscure village the child of a peasant woman....He grew up in still another village, where he worked in a carpenter's shop until he was about thirty....Then, for three years he was an itinerant preacher....He never wrote a book....He never held an office....He never had a family or owned a house....He didn't go to college....He never traveled 200 miles from the place where he was born....He did none of the things one usually associates with greatness....He had no credentials but himself....He was only 33 when public opinion turned against him... His friends ran away....He was turned over to his enemies and went through a mockery of a trial....He was nailed to a cross between two thieves....While he was dying, his executioners gambled for his clothing, the only property he had on earth....When he was dead, he was laid in a borrowed grave through the pity of a friend....Twenty centuries have come and gone, and today he is the central figure of the human race, the leader of humankind's progress....All the armies that ever marched, all the navies that ever sailed, all the governments that ever sat, all the kings that have ever reigned, put together, have not affected the lives of men and women as much as that One Solitary Life.

In other words, no one could just observe the life and teaching of Jesus. Everyone who saw him or his disciples was forced to make a judgment. Christ was a mirror into whom people looked and saw their true selves reflected. Some people did not like what they saw, and so they hated him. Jesus himself tells us that he performed works that no one else had ever done, but still "they hated me for no reason" (John 15:25).

Others, though, did not like what they saw, but this made them realize how desperately they needed him. It was these people who gathered around Jesus during his life on earth, and who formed the foundation of the Church after his resurrection.

Josephus, a Jewish historian in AD 66 wrote:"It was at that time a man appeared—if 'man' is the right word—who had all the attributes of a man but seemed to be something greater. His actions certainly were superhuman for he worked such wonderful and amazing miracles that I for one cannot regard him as a man; yet in view of his likeness to ourselves I cannot regard him as an angel either."

The fact that Jesus is hardly mentioned outside the Gospels is not surprising. When non-Christians did refer to him, they obviously saw him as a troublemaker. The writings of two famous Romans that have come down to us illustrate this:

PLINY, writing in AD 112 said the following:

In a letter to the Emperor Trajan, the Younger Pliny complains that there was a slump in the agricultural markets because people were no longer buying beasts for sacrifice. This was the fault of people called "Christians," who formed a secret society and refused to offer sacrifice to the god-emperor.

TACITUS, a Roman historian, writing early in 2nd century said this:

The Christians had been made a scapegoat for the great fire of Rome in the reign of Nero (AD 64). Their founder was a criminal who had been executed by Pontius Pilate thirty years or so earlier. Unfortunately, the death of the ringleader had not stopped the mischief!

4. "My words are spirit and they are life."

Jesus Is the Way

The life and words of Jesus have reached far beyond his native country and people. Followers of Jesus Christ believe his message is for all people and for all time. To understand this belief we need to look closely at the claims of Jesus himself who says: "I am the Way, the Truth, and the Life."

"Where do you come from?" is a question we often ask when we meet someone for the first time. It was the question about Jesus that puzzled everyone. During his public life Jesus tried to answer that question. To those who followed him, he gave this answer, "I came from the Father and have come into the world and now I leave the world to go to the Father" (John 16:28).

The Jews already possessed a deep knowledge of God. Many of Christ's sayings were already taught by the prophets and Jewish rabbis. For example, Jesus taught that when you pray you should "go to your private room and, when you have shut the door, pray to your Father who is in that secret place and your Father who sees all that is done in secret will reward you" (Matthew 6:6).

A Jewish saying, at first glance, proclaims a similar message, "He who prays within his house surrounds it with a wall that is stronger than iron." It is important to realize that in their teaching Jesus and the Jews had very much in common.

The rift between them developed only gradually, as Jesus' claims became clearer. For Jesus was not just laying down a set of laws for entry into the kingdom of God. Rather, he was claiming that his presence is the kingdom of God among men and women. Jesus came from his Father in heaven, and his coming creates, quite literally, a heaven on earth.

The condition for sharing in this "heaven on earth" is to believe in the One whom the Father has sent; to believe in his Son and what he tells us. In Christ's own words this means "changing and becoming like a little child" (Matthew 18:3). Christ is the "Way" to the Father because his life taught us how to become "children" of the Father. This is not a "Way" which can be reduced to rules and regulations. It is a life of love. But, of course, the closer the intimacy between the Father and us, his children, the greater our longing to respond to all that we experience in life in the way of love that Jesus showed us.

Jesus Is the Truth

It's always useful to have "inside information" about someone who is unfamiliar. Is that perhaps how we tend to view Jesus, someone who has come from heaven to tell us about God and what God wants us to do? What do we mean when we say that Jesus "reveals" God to us? Do we mean that because Jesus came from God, he can give us the information that we could not otherwise receive?

This is not quite the picture that comes out in the Gospels. It's not the way Jesus speaks of himself. He says, "I am the truth." Not, "I speak the truth" or "I reveal the truth," but "I am the truth."

This is not to deny that Jesus had a message to proclaim and went about Palestine proclaiming it. Of course he did. But Jesus did not only call upon men and women to believe in his message; he called upon men and women to believe in himself.

And that was something completely new. There had been prophets and teachers in the past with a message to proclaim but none of them had demanded belief in themselves. Jesus, however, slowly and gradually revealed to his disciples that he was much more than a teacher, much more than a messenger; much more than a prophet.

He had come not merely to tell men and women **about** God. He had not come merely as a messenger or as someone who could give us "inside information." In Jesus, God is actually made present to men and women.

That astounding fact shines through everything Jesus said and did. In every word and action, Jesus reveals God to us. He shows us, in human terms, what God is like. It's as though the Father is pointing to Jesus and saying, "Look! This is the kind of God I am."

In other words, we cannot separate the person of Jesus from his teachings. Every action and gesture of his is full of meaning. He is never "off duty," there is never any moment in his life when he is not showing God to us.

The miracles of Jesus speak for themselves. They are an essential part of his message. Through the miracles, men and women can see that the kingdom of God has begun.

Sent by his Father, Jesus does not merely tell us about his Father. He shows us his Father in everything he says and does.

"If you know me, you know my Father too. From this moment, you know him and have seen him."

Philip, one of his followers, said, "Lord, let us see the Father and then we shall be satisfied."

"Have I been with you all this time, Philip," said Jesus to him, "and you still do not know me? To have seen me is to have seen the Father..." (John 14:7-9).

Jesus Is the Life

All of us want to use and enjoy our lives to the full. But we can never forget that the greatest treasure we have, life itself, is a very fragile possession. The Jewish psalmist put it this way:

"For no man can buy his own ransom, or pay a price to God for his life. The ransom of his soul is beyond him. He cannot buy life without end, nor avoid coming to the grave" (Psalm 49:7-9).

In the face of death, men and women are powerless. It was this sense of powerlessness, this awareness of their own insufficiency, which intensified the Jewish desire for a savior. They longed for the gift of everlasting life.

During his public preaching Jesus said, "I have come to give them life that they might have it to the full" (John 10:10). And as time went on he began to explain to his followers exactly what he meant when he used the word "life." He told them that the only life that matters is the life that does not die—life everlasting, "I am the resurrection....If anyone believes in me even though he dies he will live, and whoever lives and believes in me will never die" (John 11:25-26).

The word used in the Russian Orthodox Church for a saint, *prepodobnia,* means "very, very like" and is a perfect description of what Jesus meant by the "true life." If we want to obtain life everlasting, we must become "very, very like" Jesus himself. And we can only do this if we receive the gift of the Holy Spirit—the Lord and Giver of life.

Throughout his time on earth, the Holy Spirit worked within Jesus, guiding and inspiring him. As John baptized Jesus "...the Holy Spirit descended on him in bodily shape, like a dove" (Luke 3:22). And when he was led into the desert to prepare for his public preaching, it was the Holy Spirit who took him there (Luke 4:1). When he eventually began to preach in Galilee, it was with the power of the Holy Spirit (Luke 4:14).

To be really like Jesus, then, we must have the Holy Spirit within us too. That is why when the time came for him to leave his apostles, Jesus promised to send the Holy Spirit. "It is for your own good that I am going," he said to them, "because unless I go, the Advocate will not come to you; but if I go I will send him to you" (John 16:7).

When the Holy Spirit came to the apostles at Pentecost, they were completely transformed. The Holy Spirit bound them more closely to Jesus by making them more like him. They were filled with new life, the life of Jesus himself, and so Saint Paul exclaimed, "I live now, not I, but Christ lives in me" (Galatians 2:20).

There is ample historical evidence that Jesus lived and preached in Palestine about 2000 years ago. There is plenty of proof too that he was a good man, that he performed miracles, that he spoke many wise words, and that he gave new hope and meaning to the lives of many people, especially those who were poor, sick, or disadvantaged.

We know, too, that his words and actions increasingly annoyed and threatened the established authorities of the time. They feared a public uprising, they feared loss of power, they feared the hypocrisy of their actions would be exposed. The result was that they executed Jesus of Nazareth. By crucifying him they hoped to solve the problem of Jesus once and for all.

It seemed as though they were successful. Once dead, he was hastily buried in a tomb. They made sure that his body couldn't be removed by his followers, and then they returned to the practice of their religious duties as the sabbath arrived. When the sabbath was over, some of the women who had followed Jesus went to the tomb with spices intending to complete the embalming of his body. In spite of the precautions of the authorities, the tomb was empty. It was empty, not because someone had taken the body, but because Jesus had risen from the dead. Jesus was alive. It was unbelievable.

- He appeared to the women, he spoke to Mary Magdalene who hurried to tell the followers of Jesus. They didn't believe her.

- He appeared to two of the disciples who were walking to the village of Emmaus, about seven miles from Jerusalem. They didn't recognize him at first because he was the last person they expected to see.

- He appeared to the eleven disciples as they gathered together in fear and uncertainty. They were terrified at first, thinking he was a ghost. But then they saw and touched the scars of his crucifixion, they watched him eat, and they realized he was a reality, a living person, raised from the dead.

Jesus had risen from the dead. Death had not destroyed him, eliminated him, or removed him from the face of the earth. Jesus is alive. That's what makes him special.

In the hours after the crucifixion of Christ, his followers were a broken, lost group. This person who had mapped out a new way of life and offered new hope and in whom they had put all their trust was now destroyed. Their world had been destroyed. They couldn't make sense of what had happened.

Then, within twelve hours, everything changed. Their leader who was dead is alive; he has been seen by at least sixteen people on five different occasions in different places. What does this mean? Fear is changed into hope and confidence. No one can dispute the fact that Jesus is alive.

When we face any change in life we begin to deal with it by continuing to function in the way that we have until the change. When that doesn't work anymore, we face tension until we accept that our previous way of coping is no longer effective. To deal with change and to grow through it, we have to find new ways of coping, new ways of living.

The followers of Jesus ran true to human behavior. Initially, they seem to have been happy to settle back into the pattern of simply being "led" by Jesus. But Jesus wouldn't allow that. To be a follower of Christ meant that they accepted his invitation to be part of his life and work in the world so that every person might come to know the promises of God and the surety of the resurrection and life after death.

Whenever Jesus was with any of his followers after his resurrection he retraced with them his teaching, his words, his actions, and the words of Scripture. Gradually, they began to see his life and his words in a new light. Although they had been with him in his years of preaching and miracle-working, they hadn't realized the implications. They hadn't realized what it all meant.

Only on looking back, following the living proof of the resurrection, could they begin to grasp the reality of the life of Jesus of Nazareth and the reality of what the coming of the Messiah really meant.

What makes Jesus special?

That very same day, two of them were on their way to a village called Emmaus, seven miles from Jerusalem, and they were talking together about all that had happened. Now as they talked this over, Jesus himself came up and walked by their side; but something prevented them from recognizing him. He said to them, "What matters are you discussing as you walk along?" They stopped short, their faces downcast.

Then one of them, called Cleopas, answered him, "You must be the only person staying in Jerusalem who does not know the things that have been happening there these last few days." "What things?" he asked. "All about Jesus of Nazareth," they answered, "who proved he was a great prophet by the things he said and did in the sight of God and of the whole people; and how our chief priests and our leaders handed him over to be sentenced to death, and had him crucified. Our own hope had been that he would be the one to set Israel free. And this is not all; two whole days have gone by since it all happened; and some women from our group have astounded us: they went back to the tomb in the early morning, and when they did not find the body, they came back to tell us they had seen a vision of angels who declared he was alive. Some of our friends went to the tomb and found everything exactly as the women had reported, but of him they saw nothing" (Luke 24:13-24).

My words are Spirit and they are life

The full significance of the death and resurrection of Jesus is hinted at in John's Gospel. John tells us that as Jesus died on the cross a soldier pierced his side with a sword and "immediately there came out blood and water." The blood and water are a sign of the outpouring of the love of Jesus. This outflow is a sign of the Spirit of Jesus in which we can all share. And then, after his resurrection, the first act of Jesus is to breathe on his followers. As he did so, he said,

"Receive the Holy Spirit.
For those whose sins you forgive,
they are forgiven."
(John 20:22-23)

In giving us his life and in sharing his Spirit with us, Jesus unites us with himself at the deepest possible level. At Mass, in the Eucharistic Prayer, we pray that we may become "one body, one Spirit in Christ."

The work of the Spirit of Jesus Christ, symbolized so powerfully in the life-blood and breath of Jesus, is to bring all people into harmony with God. Fifty days after the resurrection other symbols of God's Spirit were used. Christ's followers heard "what sounded like a powerful wind from heaven" and "something appeared to them like tongues of fire" (Acts 2:1-3). But whatever form the Spirit took, its effects were the same. The effect was to bring people together so that, on the day of Pentecost, everyone, of whatever language, could understand what Christ's followers were saying. When he died, when he gave himself up completely, Jesus released his Spirit in order to *unite* us.

In his death and resurrection, Jesus released a most powerful force for the re-creation of our world. Of course, the work of the Holy Spirit will only be complete when we are all gathered together as one body in the kingdom of God. Meanwhile, we follow Christ in his struggle to bring all people to God. And we can follow Jesus in his work and in his prayer because we share in his Holy Spirit. As we will see later in *Your Faith*, the Holy Spirit has been breathed into our own hearts so that we can show others that Jesus is alive and also share his life with others.

The work of the Holy Spirit is summarized by Saint Paul in his Letter to the Romans. Saint Paul tells us how the Spirit, poured out in the death of Jesus and breathed into us in his resurrection, unites us with Jesus Christ and enables us to recognize God as our most loving Father. The Spirit of God has been given to us, yet there is a struggle before the Spirit's work is complete in us and in the world.

"Everyone moved by the Spirit is a son of God. The Spirit you received is not the spirit of slaves bringing fear into your lives again; it is the spirit of sons and it makes us cry out, 'Abba, Father!' The Spirit himself and our spirit bear united witness that we are children of God. And if we are children we are heirs as well: heirs of God and co-heirs with Christ, sharing his sufferings so as to share his glory.

I think that what we suffer in this life can never be compared to the glory, as yet unrevealed, which is waiting for us. The whole creation is eagerly waiting for God to reveal his sons. It was not for any fault on the part of creation that it was made unable to attain its purpose, it was made so by God; but creation still retains the hope of being freed, like us, from its slavery to decadence, to enjoy the same freedom and glory as the children of God. From the beginning till now the entire creation, as we know, has been groaning in one great act of giving birth; and not only creation, but all of us who possess the first fruits of the Spirit, we too groan inwardly as we wait for our bodies to be set free. For we must be content to hope that we shall be saved—our salvation is not in sight, we should not have to be hoping for it if it were—but, as I say, we must hope to be saved since we are not saved yet—it is something we must wait for with patience."

Paul to the Romans 8:14-25

The significance of the death & resurrection of Jesus

The miracles of Jesus

Throughout the Gospels Jesus is shown healing the sick, curing lepers, the blind, the lame, the deaf—even raising the dead to life. It would be a great mistake to underrate the importance and the significance of these miraculous actions.

Jesus did not perform them simply to add authority to his teaching or to convince unbelievers. Nor did he perform them simply to demonstrate that he had special power. There is no hint of the showmanship about them. They are not stunts performed to astonish his audience.

Far from using his miracles to impress large crowds, Jesus performed most of them in the presence of only a few people. And he frequently forbade his disciples to tell anyone about the miracles they had seen. This in itself is an indication that the miracles had a more profound purpose. Another indication is that in the Gospel of John the miracles are always called signs.

Signs of what? Jesus answers that question for us, "The very works that I am doing bear witness that the Father has sent me" (John 5:36).

The miracles, in other words, are signs of his mission; signs that the kingdom of God is present and at work in the world. They are signs of God's love for men and women; signs that Jesus has come to free men and women from the sin which has brought with it death, sickness, and disease.

5. The Spirit will teach

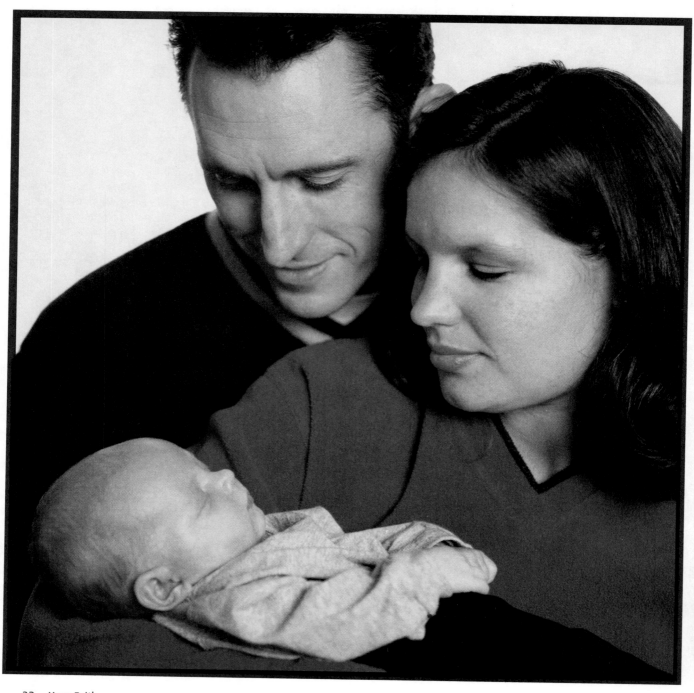

you everything

The resurrection of Jesus Christ struck the followers of Jesus like a burst of lightning. To begin with they were blinded. They didn't understand what was happening. They were rather like any one of us after a blinding flash or an automobile accident. Finding ourselves in a state of shock, we take a long time to piece together what's happened. It's a long, sometimes painstaking, process.

On their road to recovery and in their search for understanding of what had happened, the first followers of Jesus enjoyed the support of the Holy Spirit, promised by Jesus.

Jesus had told them:

"The Advocate, the Holy Spirit, whom the Father will send in my name, will teach you everything and remind you of all I have said to you" (John 14:26).

It would be a mistake, however, to imagine that the Holy Spirit gave full knowledge and understanding to the followers of Jesus immediately. We have only to look at the followers of Jesus today to realize that we have a long way to go before we all come together as one in our understanding and response to the words of Jesus.

It's as though the sudden burst of light at the resurrection of Jesus still blinds and confuses us. Christ's followers through the ages have struggled and will continue to wrestle with the full meaning of the life and teaching of Jesus Christ.

The first inspired followers of Jesus, under the apostles specially named by Jesus, continued the work and teaching of Jesus in two ways. Each of these two ways is equally important.

1 They passed on the words of Jesus by word of mouth—in the Tradition of the Church.

2 They passed on the words of Jesus in written form—in the Scriptures of the Church.

The Life-Giving Spirit in the Church

Following the resurrection of Jesus, the first thing his disciples did under the influence of the Holy Spirit was to **preach**—to tell others about what had happened. Peter concludes his first sermon with the words: "For this reason the whole House of Israel can be certain that God has made this Jesus whom you crucified both Lord and Christ." As a result of his words many, we are told, were added to the number of followers.

The words of Jesus were also recalled and celebrated in their **liturgy** or worship of his disciples. They came together for what they called "the breaking of bread" when they recalled the words of Jesus and did as he had instructed on the night before he died. The words and work of Jesus were continued, too, in **the teaching of the apostles** as they faced new situations and problems. One of the most serious difficulties within the early Church, for example, was the question of Jewish observance: should all converts to the new Christian faith continue to observe Jewish customs? Such customs were a burden to non-Jews—a major source of discouragement to prospective converts. In resolving this, Peter (as a result of some pressure from Paul) took the lead. He told the others: "I remembered that the Lord had said, 'John baptized with water, but you will be baptized with the Holy Spirit.' I realized then that God was giving them (the non-Jews) the identical thing he gave to us when we believed in the Lord Jesus Christ; and who was I to stand in God's way?"

In so many ways, then, the teaching of Jesus was continued by word of mouth. We call this "word of mouth" transmitting of the Gospel the TRADITION of the Church.

Next time you go to Sunday Mass take a look at the people around you. What are they like? If yours is an average parish community your fellow worshipers will be a very mixed bunch indeed. They'll be far more varied than a football crowd or a cinema audience.

There will be people of all ages present, from babes in arms to very elderly retirees. They will be from widely differing backgrounds: some well-to-do, others barely scraping along. There will be differences of class, race, and nationality. They will have brought with them very different preoccupations, problems and difficulties, hopes, dreams, and ambitions and fears and anxieties.

Yet the very fact that they have gathered together for worship shows that, in spite of their natural differences, there is something which unites them and binds them together.

What binds them together is not, in fact, something; it is someone. This truth is expressed very clearly in one of the greetings at the beginning of Mass:

"The grace of our Lord Jesus Christ and the love of God and the fellowship of the Holy Spirit be with you all."

"The fellowship of the Holy Spirit...." It is here that our unity as Christians lies. For the Church is people—people united, first and foremost, by the Holy Spirit who dwells in their hearts.

Sometimes when we talk about the Church we think of buildings or of a large organization or of the pope and the hierarchy. These have their place, but what makes the Church to be the Church, is, before anything else, the Holy Spirit in people's hearts.

The Life-Giving Spirit

Although the people of the Old Testament did not fully understand the nature of God, they nevertheless had a vivid awareness of the role of God's Spirit in their lives. Their understanding can best be summed up in the phrase, "Life-giving Spirit."

They looked upon the Spirit as the source of all life in God's creation. But the Spirit of God was not only the source of natural life. The Jews realized, because God had revealed it to them, that the Spirit was also the source of men's and women's moral life.

Those human beings who were pleasing to God were those who enjoyed the gift of God's Spirit. They knew, too, that God's Spirit would only be fully poured out in the time of Christ. Their experience of men's and women's sinfulness led them to the conclusion that human beings were hopelessly sinful and evil if left on their own. Only when God's Spirit was poured out all over the world would things change.

The Spirit and Jesus

The Spirit of God was always with God's Son, Jesus Christ. His very conception in the womb of his mother, Mary, was, as Luke tells us in his Gospel, due to the overshadowing of Mary by the Holy Spirit of God. Jesus was anointed for his saving mission as our Messiah when he was baptized by John in the river Jordan.

Yet Jesus Christ, as man, could only send the Spirit to us, his brothers and sisters, when he had risen from the dead and ascended to his Father. He told us that unless he went back to his Father, the Paraclete (the Spirit) would not come.

In other words, the Spirit of God could only come upon all men and women when our leader, Jesus Christ, was reunited with his Father. This is why the Spirit comes; to unite us to Christ and so to God our Father. The Holy Spirit, the Spirit of God, is our life. We share the life of Jesus Christ because we share his Spirit whom he sent to us.

The Spirit—The Soul of the Church

Just as the different parts of our body share our life, so we and all our fellow Christians share the same Spirit, the same life of Christ. This, as we have already said, is what is meant by the phrase used at the beginning of Mass, "The fellowship of the Holy Spirit."

This, then, is the importance of the Holy Spirit; he is the ever-present source of life within us. He dwells within us, helping us to grow closer and closer to Jesus Christ. We can be confident in the reality of this if we look at the lives of the earliest disciples. Even when they had Jesus with them, they were very weak in faith. In the Gospels, we see Jesus rebuking them repeatedly for their lack of faith and understanding; it's a theme which runs right through all the Gospels.

We can recall, too, their failure at the crucifixion, the betrayal of Judas who was a chosen apostle, Peter's denial, the wholesale desertion of Christ by the others. In spite of their closeness to Jesus, the weakness of their faith and their limited understanding shows up.

Yet look at what happens after the resurrection. The apostles spent the rest of their lives preaching about Jesus. They gave up their lives for him, willingly. Surely they had strong faith and a deep understanding then.

But this strong faith, this deep understanding, came to them only after Jesus had left them. What happened to transform this group of frightened, inhibited men into a force which was to take the message of Jesus Christ to the whole world?

What happened was the coming of the Holy Spirit. In fact, the apostles only fully believed, only fully understood, when Jesus Christ had returned in glory to his Father and had sent the Holy Spirit upon them as he had promised.

"It is for your own good that I am going because unless I go the Advocate will not come to you; but if I do go I will send him to you... and when the Spirit of truth comes he will lead you to the complete truth" (John 16).

At the time the apostles couldn't understand that at all. How could any arrangement be better than having Jesus there with them? It was only after they had received the Holy Spirit that they realized what Jesus meant. Only then did they realize that although he was no longer physically present he was present in a much more wonderful way—in his Spirit. And that presence transformed them, they became different people.

And that presence transforms us and makes us different too. The same Spirit who came to the apostles on the day of Pentecost dwells in each one of us. It is through him that we are able to believe in Jesus Christ, love Christ, and have confidence in Christ. The Holy Spirit lives in us, uniting us to Christ and pouring his love upon us. That's not simply a pious thought; we have the word of Jesus that it is a fact.

The Spirit in the Church

The Spirit doesn't just live in us as individuals. After the resurrection and ascension of Jesus, the Holy Spirit descended on his followers as a body. It was in their coming together for prayer, for the breaking of bread in the Eucharist and for sharing their understanding of the life and words of Jesus that the first disciples grew in their faith in God. And the Tradition that began in the teaching of the apostles continues to the present day. It may be tempting at times to "go it alone" in our faith; but it is in the community of the Church—the Body of Christ—that the life of the Spirit is most certainly found.

The Life-Giving Spirit in the Scriptures

As the first followers of Jesus died (many through martyrdom) they began to put down in writing their belief in Jesus. The first person to do this was Paul of Tarsus, who wrote a number of letters to his converts that survive to the present day. More importantly, others began to set down the life and teaching of Jesus in an ordered form. These books which tell us of the life of Jesus are the four gospels. The gospels, with the letters of Paul and a number of other writings, are known as the New Testament—the SCRIPTURES—which all followers of Jesus Christ read and reverence in our growth in love and knowledge of Jesus Christ.

These two ways of continuing the message of Jesus Christ—the Scriptures and the Tradition of the Church—are compared by the Church to two streams which "flow from the same divine well-spring, come together in some fashion to form one thing, and move towards the same goal. Sacred Scripture is the speech of God as it is put down in writing under the breath of the Holy Spirit. And Tradition transmits in its entirety the Word of God which has been entrusted to the apostles by Christ the Lord and the Holy Spirit" (Vatican II).

The Holy Spirit, then, keeps alive the words and life of Jesus Christ. Whenever the word of Jesus is spoken or read by his followers the power of God is breathed into those words by the Holy Spirit—the same Spirit whom Jesus breathed into his followers after his resurrection. It will be helpful to look more closely at how the Spirit continues to give life to the Church when Christ's followers are brought together by the words of Jesus Christ.

It is usual to read a book alone. We settle into an armchair or struggle to get a seat on a bus and cut ourselves off from the rest of the world so that we can absorb ourselves into what we are reading.

It is impossible, however, to read properly the Scriptures which make up the New Testament in such a way. When we read the gospels attentively, the words of Jesus engage us and we are caught up by them. We are lifted up to a closer relationship with God. This is the work of the Holy Spirit who helps us grow in our understanding of the words of Jesus—just as the same Holy Spirit inspired their writing. As we are taken up into the life of God we are also drawn more deeply into the community of the Church whose early members first wrote the gospels. There is a sense in which we cannot read the gospels entirely on our own.

The "inspiration" by the Holy Spirit doesn't mean that God dictated the Scriptures with a loud voice from heaven. God's activity always comes in a human way. He works through the circumstances of our everyday lives. And the New Testament writings, including the gospels, were written by human beings in a human manner but in such a way that God is their author.

Stage 1—The life of Jesus

When Jesus was born in Bethlehem, God became man. The men and women who saw Jesus Christ saw him in a human form that helped them understand what God was really like. But from the beginning, he called some of his followers to be special observers, special witnesses, of these important years. These were apostles.

They saw him show compassion to the poor and to sinners. They saw him heal the sick. They heard him speak in a simple language that everyone could understand. They were the special witnesses. They knew that Jesus Christ had come to bring a message of salvation to all people.

Stage 2—The preaching of the apostles

"Go out to the whole world; proclaim the Good News to all creation." The apostles were now well equipped to carry out this last command of Jesus and, like him, they did it in a simple manner. Their intimate knowledge of Christ meant they could give their hearers a vivid picture of his life and teachings. They could describe his miracles in minute detail and repeat his stories and teachings accurately. But that was not enough. How could they best show that these stories and miracles pointed to something deeper?

Gradually, the apostles put their knowledge of Jesus into an orderly scheme. In their preaching they grouped miracles together to show how everyone could share in this new life. They selected parables which urged their listeners to follow Christ. And so we can see an important fact emerging about the formation of the gospels. Even before the first gospels were written, the life and teaching of Jesus was being put into an accepted order. And this was being done by the apostles, those who really knew Christ.

Stage 3—The evangelists

The Jewish memory was extremely retentive. We cannot easily forget repetitive TV commercials because the order of the words is always the same. The same was true of the early Jewish converts.

Once the apostles had grouped the miracles, teachings, and parables of Jesus into a set order, their listeners would not easily forget. The words of the apostles would be firmly imprinted in their memory. This helps us to understand the part played by the gospel writers.

They did not write a book in the sense that we speak of a modern author writing a book. They put into writing what was at first passed on by word of mouth. Their work—and this is their great gift to us—brings us into direct contact with the preaching of the apostles, the official witnesses of the life of Jesus.

Where did the gospels come from?

For the first thirty-five years after Jesus' death, the gospels didn't exist. Why was that? What was happening during those first days of the Church?

As long as the apostles were still alive, there was no thought of a written book. The apostles had lived with Christ; they had known him intimately. They had seen him live, die, and rise from the dead. In fact, the apostles have been described as the "living books" on which the Christian message was written.

There were other reasons too.

- The age in which the first Christians lived was a non-literary one. Mass-produced printing was a long way off.

- A single sheet of papyrus cost more than a worker's daily wage.

- The first Christians were, for the most part, poor and uncultured. They could not read.

- The Jews preferred to commit knowledge to memory rather than write it down.

Those first thirty-five years, however, were not years of inactivity, for over this period the gospels were beginning to take shape in a very real way. There were three stages in this process:

The two ways of continuing the message of Jesus Christ— the Scriptures and the Tradition of the Church—are like two streams which flow from the same divine well-spring. They are like two candles which, through the ages, continue to reveal the light which is Jesus Christ.

The calendar

Many events in life are difficult to remember. It can be hard to place them exactly in their proper order. Often it is helpful if we can arrange them around the more important events that we will never forget: Was it before or after we got married? Was that the year that we went to Australia? Was that the year the pope came to the United States? It was a sound idea, based on that human habit, that made a monk called Denis the Little want to adjust the calendar.

Until the sixth century, events were placed in history around the date of the founding of the city of Rome. Denis wanted to change that and arrange everything around the year of Christ's birth, the most important event in the history of the world.

Denis's idea was a good one and we have become accustomed to referring to things happening "before Christ" or "after Christ." There was only one unfortunate error; Denis miscalculated the exact year of the birth of Christ. This doesn't really matter, but it does mean that if we want to be precise we would have to say that Christ was born somewhere between the years 6-4 BC.

Since it is known from other sources that King Herod (who massacred the Holy Innocents) died in the year that Denis had calculated to be 4 BC, we would have to say that Christ must have been born before this. Again, if we are trying to be precise, we would also have to say that Christ probably died in the year which the calendar gives as AD 30, having begun his ministry a few years earlier.

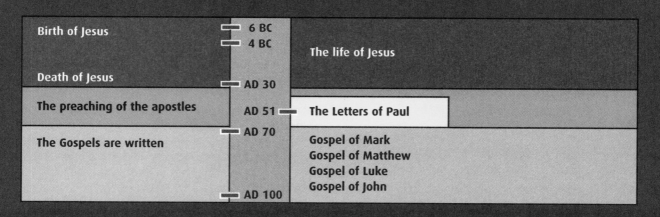

Birth of Jesus	6 BC	
	4 BC	The life of Jesus
Death of Jesus	AD 30	
The preaching of the apostles	AD 51	The Letters of Paul
The Gospels are written	AD 70	Gospel of Mark Gospel of Matthew Gospel of Luke Gospel of John
	AD 100	

Who were the gospels for?

Did you know that the Gospel of Matthew and the Gospel of Mark were each written with a completely different type of reader in mind? Matthew's gospel was written primarily for Jewish converts, while Mark's was written for Romans. This simple fact is a strong hint to us that it's important to be careful to avoid approaching each of the four gospels in the same way.

The Gospel of Mark

There is an early Christian tradition that Mark was a follower of Saint Peter in Rome. His gospel was probably written there shortly before or after the death of Peter. It is thought that Mark's was the first of the gospels to be written (about AD 64-67). Mark never saw Jesus so it is likely that he used Peter's accounts of the words of Jesus in his gospel.

This gospel was written primarily for Roman converts who wanted a permanent record of the life of Jesus as it had been taught to them by Saint Peter. Because it was for Romans, Mark's gospel contains many explanations of Jewish customs. It also explains the meaning of Aramaic words and expressions. The Old Testament is hardly ever quoted. Mark concentrates on Jesus as the Son of God rather than as the Savior promised in the Old Testament.

Mark's gospel is noted for the miracles it records. It is more a gospel of action than of words. It is the shortest of the four and can be read at one sitting.

The Gospel of Matthew

This gospel has been described as the greatest book ever written. It is certainly the most familiar and the most popular of the four gospels.

Written with a fine sense of order and balance, it presents Jesus as a great teacher who fulfills the Old Testament prophecies; the promised Messiah who completes God's plan. It was written primarily for Jewish converts and therefore contains many references to the Old Testament. It was probably composed about AD 70.

This gospel has been called the most important single document of the Christian faith because it contains the fullest account of the life and teaching of Jesus. It is also the most frequently used in the teaching and worship of the Church.

Matthew was a painstaking teacher. Unlike Mark, who was often content to state the bare facts about Jesus, Matthew explains at length the significance of Jesus and his teaching. Because he is speaking with a Jewish audience in mind, he plans his writing around five great discourses of Christ which are seen as the equivalent of the five books of the old law.

The Gospel of Luke

As well as a gospel, Luke wrote the Acts of the Apostles, making him the author of just over a quarter of the entire New Testament. His writings describe fully the beginnings of Christianity from the earliest moments of Christ's life to his ascension and beyond to the years when the community of the Church was growing and spreading.

Luke is the only Gentile writer in the New Testament, and it may be that this explains his interest and concern for the outsider and the care with which he records Christ's dealings with all those who were in some way outside the community.

Luke presents a picture of Christ and his teaching which has immediate appeal even on the human level alone. His gospel was primarily intended for Christians already familiar with the gospel teaching, but it also seeks to attract non-Christians. It was written in Greek and has an educated style. It emphasises that Jesus is the Savior of all women and men and stresses the compassion of Jesus for the poor and the outcast. It has been called the gospel of social justice.

The Gospel of John

The Gospel of John shows a marked difference from the other three gospels. All four evangelists select their material to suit their purpose but this selection is most evident in John. John's gospel was written in Greek about AD 100 and bears the characteristics of an old man's reflections on past events, delving into their deeper meaning. The purpose of this gospel is "that you may believe that Jesus is the Christ the Son of God...."

Although John's gospel carefully places events in correct chronological order, it would be a mistake to think of it as straight reporting. With this gospel more than the others, we have to read between the lines for the full meaning. This is one of the most inspiring parts of the New Testament and one of the best loved. This is partly due to the fact that it is a very personal statement of faith in Christ. John the Evangelist knew how to transmit his own living memories, and his love for Christ is obvious on every page.

The Church has always reverenced this document as the work of John the Apostle, although the gospel as we have it would appear to be the work of his disciples who actually wrote down what John had taught and dictated.

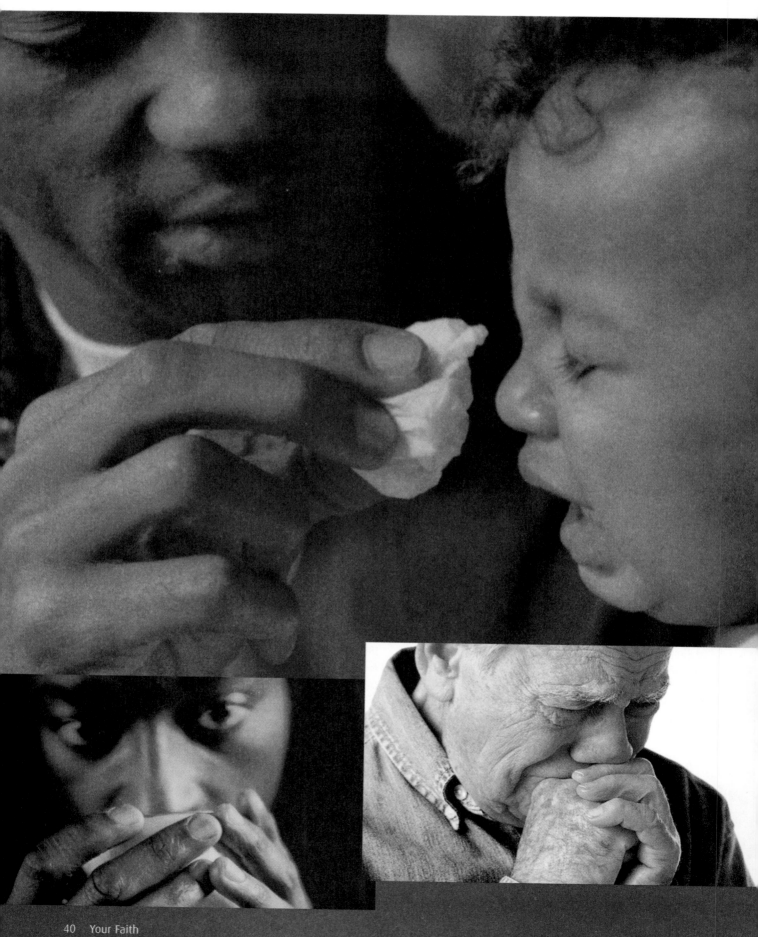

6. The Spirit for Our Wounded World

Once the followers of Jesus realized, as a result of the resurrection, that Christ really was the Son of God, they were facing a new and serious dilemma; how would they cope with this information? How would anyone cope with such information? It was great news, exciting and encouraging, but it was also overwhelming. They were ordinary people, not scholars, religious, or unusually gifted. What could they do with the Good News which they accepted as fact?

One of the important points of the Good News is, of course, that God is in control of his world; he knows what is best for his people. And so, true to his word, God acts. Christ, in his appearances after his resurrection, helped his followers to make sense of what had happened:

"He then opened their minds to understand the scriptures, and he said to them, 'So you see how it is written that the Christ would suffer and on the third day rise from the dead.' "

He reassured them that a change of heart (repentance) would ensure a new beginning,

"and that in his name (Christ), repentance for the forgiveness of sins would be preached to all the nations, beginning from Jerusalem. You are witnesses to this" **(Luke 24:45-48).**

And finally, he promised that he would be with them always,

"Go, therefore, make disciples of all the nations; baptize them in the name of the Father and of the Son and of the Holy Spirit, and teach them to observe all the commands I gave you. And know that I am with you always; yes, to the end of time" (Matthew 28:19-20).

"As the Father sent me, so I am sending you" (John 2:21).

The Father sent his Son into the world to show us once and for all the true nature of God—that he is a God of love, not a God of law. That Spirit of God which had been with Jesus in his life on earth is promised to all who believe and accept the Good News of the kingdom of God. They will never be alone because the Spirit of God will be intimately involved in all that they say and do in his name. This is how the kingdom of God is formed on earth; by those actions of the Holy Spirit in and through the people of God.

What's the matter with our world?

Original Sin

Saint Paul speaks of the existence of original sin in his Letter to the Romans. Original sin is the basis for all sin in the world. It is the foundation of the absence or denial of God in the lives of men and women.

In Genesis, we read the story of Adam, the first man, a representative of the human race. As our representative, Adam was created holy and a perfect example of a complete and just human being. But Adam chose to follow his own choices, his own ways, rather than the ways of his Creator. His will was superimposed on the will of God and so disorder, death, and deterioration entered the world.

In sending us his Son, Jesus Christ, God offers to all men and women a chance of a new creation. A creation which is once more holy, just, and eternally life-giving. Jesus Christ revealed the healing, guiding hand of God in our world and offered it to all who would accept it. The pride, the desire for self-worship and a rejection of God's ways recur, but we know that we are not expected to overcome these hurdles, these hardships, alone.

Jesus Christ told us of the kingdom of God. He told us the Good News that we are redeemed, sanctified, and made one with our heavenly Father in and through our baptism.

Clearly, in spite of this new birth, we are still inclined to sin and self-worship. We are still drawn towards turning inwards and focusing on our own values and desires. As long as we live we rely constantly on God's healing Spirit to renew us, restore us, and help us overcome our failings so that we can live our new life as a true reflection of Christ's life.

The magnetic pull of original sin remains with us as long as we live, but the grace and strength of the Spirit of Christ is always powerful enough to overcome it. We are dependent on God. We are created and we exist through his loving creativity. All life and love is a gift. In living in unity with God we find a completeness which is not to be found elsewhere. That is our faith. That is Christ's promise. Original sin no longer has any power over us as long as we acknowledge our dependence on God.

What's the matter with our world?

We can put people on the moon; we can fly the Atlantic in a few hours; we can watch events on the other side of the world as they happen. In the field of technology, men and women have made tremendous progress. But when it comes to the business of living together in peace, of caring and loving, we seem to have made little or no progress at all. In some respects, the ways in which we hurt and destroy one another seem to have got worse. At times it can feel as though we are going backwards, not forwards. And the really numbing thing about the evil we see all around us is the feeling that we, as individuals, can do little or nothing about it all. We feel helpless.

What's the matter with us?

Yet the disease is not only in the world around us, it is also in ourselves. We, too, do our share of harm to others. We are selfish and cruel. We fail to love, day in and day out.

The inescapable conclusion is that there is something wrong with men and women. Somehow, somewhere along the line, we got involved with sin. There is no need, at this point, to look back at the beginnings of human history to find out precisely how we got into this situation. The important point is that this situation is a fact. It is plain for all to see.

If we have any doubts about our world's need for redemption, for a fresh start, we need look no further than today's news bulletins. If we have any doubt about our own personal need of redemption we need look no further than our own hearts.

Why did Jesus come?

"The Son of man has come to seek out and save what was lost." The idea of being "lost" is a very good description of what sin means. When we are lost we have left the right road; we're wandering aimlessly with no sense of purpose or direction.

Wars, massacres, cruelty, exploitation, race hatred, injustice, crime...our newspapers and TV screens are full of all these things. We can't get away from them.

Men and women turned away from God are lost. They have broken off contact with God who alone gives meaning and purpose to life. They become rather like an aircraft pilot trying to land in fog, having lost contact with ground control. Unable to re-establish contact, the pilot only wanders further and further away from the true destination.

If men and women are to find their way again it must be shown to them. We must be put once more on the right road. This can only be done by someone who knows the way, someone who has not lost contact; someone, in other words, who knows no sin, whose vision is clear and unclouded.

Jesus came to do that for us. He came to re-establish for us a true and loving relationship with God, his Father. Through Jesus it becomes possible for us to break out of the net of sin in which we have become imprisoned.

A shattering truth

Jesus, as he himself said, came to seek out and save what was lost. That simple phrase contains a profound truth, a truth which stands at the very heart of the Christian message; the truth that God gives himself to us.

It is men and women who have failed. It is men and women who have destroyed the relationship between God and themselves. But God does not wait for the guilty to come to him to be reconciled. He goes out to them. He gives himself to them. God, in Jesus, seeks them out.

And there are no strings attached; no conditions laid down. God, quite simply, gives himself to men and women; a free gift of himself.

This shattering truth sets Christianity apart from other world religions. It stands our usual way of thinking about religion on its head. Men and women have always thought that they must remove the guilt they feel before God by their own unaided efforts; thinking that they must do something in order that God will look kindly on them.

The truth is almost exactly opposite; God already looks kindly on them. This is overwhelming; so overwhelming that when they heard this, when they heard that God had given himself to men and women, they did not accept him.

The Spirit for Our Wounded World

Why does God allow suffering in the world?
This is the commonest objection to belief in God, and there is no slick answer to it. A starting point is to ask, "What sort of world would it be in which suffering was totally eliminated?" Clearly it would be a very different world from the one we live in now. First of all, the physical environment would have to be different. A world in which, for example, there could be no earthquakes, no drought, no floods, no disease would have to be a physically different world from the one we live in. Is such a physically different world possible? Modern science seems to suggest that it isn't. The basic laws of physics are so finely tuned that even a minute change in them would reduce the world to chaos. If this is the case then it looks as though the laws which make it possible for us to exist at all are the same laws which create the conditions in which suffering is possible.

But even if the physical world could be changed so as to eliminate the possibility of diseases and natural disasters, that would not solve the problem. There still remains the suffering which human beings inflict on themselves and on one another. To change that would mean changing people. Their freedom of choice would have to be destroyed, for people cannot have true freedom unless the possibility of misusing it is there.

Would it be a better world if we had no free choice; if we were all programmed automatons? Would such an existence, with all suffering eliminated, be worth having?

Suffering, then, seems to be a consequence of the way things are. But it would be a mistake to think that God is indifferent to suffering—or worse—that he deliberately inflicts it. We believe that God has revealed himself in the person of Jesus Christ. And in Jesus Christ, God has subjected himself to the consequences of the universe he has created. When Jesus died in terrible agony on the cross he showed himself to be at one with suffering humanity. He also showed that suffering can be transformed into life; that evil can be overcome by love. This helps us to glimpse the meaning of suffering; that it is not all a futile waste.

"I have come so that they may have life and have it to the full."

(John 10:10)

What did Jesus do for us?

Jesus made it possible for us to stop being the kind of people we are and to become the kind of person he is, the kind of person we were created to be; a reflection of our heavenly Father. That is what redemption means.

- Jesus lived in the world as one of us.

- He was fully human.

- He shared with men and women the human condition which involves suffering and death.

- But where others sinned, he remained sinless.

- Where others failed to love, he loved completely, unconditionally.

- Where others did only their own will, he carried out the will of his Father.

In everything he did, Jesus showed us what it means to live with and for God. Jesus, though, did not come simply as an example which we could follow. He did not come simply to be the perfect model of someone who lived a fully human life as God intended it to be lived. He came to make it possible for us to overcome the suffocating power of sin. He came to make it possible for us to change.

Jesus made it possible for us to change by his death and resurrection. We can never hope to understand that fully and that's why we speak of the mystery of our redemption. All we can do is to try to get as near the truth as possible.

Why did Jesus die on the cross?

In trying to understand the answer to this question we must reject, right from the start, any false idea of God the Father as a harsh and cruel judge who demanded that his Son should suffer and die to make up for the sins of men and women. It is love, not some abstract idea of justice, which provides the key to our understanding. "God loved the world so much that he gave his only Son, so that everyone who believes in him may not die but have eternal life. For God did not send his Son into the world to be its judge but to be its Savior" (John 3:16-17).

Jesus suffered because suffering is an inevitable part of human existence; no one is free from it. He suffered, too, because what he was, what he taught, and what he did provoked resistance and hostility from sinful people. It was men and women who refused to accept Jesus and his teaching, men and women who put Jesus to death.

Jesus could have avoided the cross, he could have run away, but he didn't. Instead he remained true to his Father, true to the Spirit within him, true to the message of love which he had come to bring. In other words, he remained faithful to his Father's will, and his faithfulness brought him to death.

Where does the resurrection fit in?

When Peter and the other apostles received the gift of the Holy Spirit and started to preach the good news of the Gospel, the central point of their message was the resurrection of Jesus from the dead. The resurrection is the basis of our Christian faith. Why is it so important?

It would be a mistake to think of the resurrection merely as a proof that Jesus was God. The significance of it goes much deeper than that. Saint Paul gives us some idea of its significance when he says, "...if Christ has not been raised, you are still in your sins."

The resurrection is the completion of the sacrifice Jesus made on the cross. Because Jesus remained true to his Father's word, his Father raised him from the dead to a new life of glory. Jesus, with the Spirit of God within him, is reunited with his Father forever. And we, who share in his Spirit, become his brothers and sisters. He has reunited our fallen human race with God. Our redemption, our new beginning, is achieved.

Jesus–the light of the world

There is nothing so discouraging as being told constantly to "try harder." Our driving instructor tells us to "try harder" and we find ourselves driving into the lamppost instead; we "try harder" to be patient with someone whom we find difficult and end up saying the worst possible things. Being told to "try harder" generally ties us up in knots as we wrestle with our weaknesses and anxieties.

One of the consoling things about Jesus is that he never told us to "try harder." He never said that, in our lives, we needed more effort. However, he did tell us that, in our lives, we needed more light. That is why he invites us to follow him in his path to happiness. For Jesus' vision of that path is clear and unclouded. In following him we see life in a new light and this, more than anything, will change our behavior and the way we act. What are the principal ways in which our ways of thinking and acting are changed in the light of the teaching of Jesus Christ?

■ The teaching of Jesus shows us that religion is not a set of laws, but is a relationship. It is always tempting to reduce religion to rules. This was a problem with the Jewish religion at the time of Jesus. Some rules are an essential part of any human society and Jesus himself emphasized the importance of the Law in providing us with boundaries for our behavior. The relationship between God and ourselves, however, like the relationship between parent and child, is not founded on rules but on trust or what Jesus calls "faith." Rules and laws can never be a substitute for faith. Jesus came among us, above all, to open our eyes to God's trust in us and assures us that true happiness is to be found in placing our faith in him.

■ The teaching of Jesus shows us the dignity of each one of us. This is an area where so many people live in darkness—they are blind to the beauty of themselves and of others. For example, Jesus reminds us how God clothes the wild flowers growing in the field which are there today and thrown into the furnace tomorrow so "will he not much more look after you, you who have so little faith?" He tells us, "See that you never despise any of these little ones... it is never the will of your Father in heaven that one of these little ones should be lost." And Jesus reassures us that those who follow his word are not his "servants" but "friends" who live in the same love of the Father as he himself.

This puts our understanding of the dignity of ourselves and of others in a wholly new light. This is why the Church places such importance on the dignity of every person from the moment of conception to the moment of death. It is the basis of the Church's insistence on the importance of individual conscience and the responsibility we have for informing it, for conscience "is our most secret core and our sanctuary. There we are alone with God whose voice echoes in our depths" (Pope Pius XII).

■ The teaching of Jesus gives us a sense of direction and purpose. Without help and training, a blind person will bump and bang into every obstacle in his or her path and be badly hurt. Similarly, without the light of God's word we will damage one another and the world in which we live. Light enables us to see where we are going. And so Jesus tells us:

"I am the light of the world; anyone who follows me will not be walking in the dark but will have the light of life" (John 8:12).

In the light of the words of Jesus every action of ours takes on new meaning. Each action contributes to the building up of the kingdom of God in this world and moves us towards God, who lives in eternal light. And so we can look forward to the day when, at last, we see God face to face and enjoy true happiness forever.

At the beginning of his gospel, John refers to the "darkness" of this world (John 1:4). Jesus himself often referred to it and, at the hour of his death, we are told that "darkness came over the whole land until the ninth hour...when Jesus cried out in a loud voice saying, 'Father, into your hands I commit my spirit' " (Luke 23:44-46).

Jesus certainly did not escape the sin and suffering of this wounded world. He was crucified by it. Yet in his life and at the moment of his death he shed light on the way to a solution. In the giving up of his Spirit, which is released for every person to share, he invites us into a new relationship with his Father; he helps us to recognize the dignity of every person and he gives us new purpose. This new vision proclaimed by Jesus Christ is infinitely more effective than any attempts on our part to "try harder" in the reconstruction of this world and the building up of the kingdom of God.

7. The Spirit of God has made a home in you

Throughout his life and his teaching, Jesus makes it very clear that God is our deeply loving parent who longs for a full and complete relationship with us, founded and centered upon mutual love and confidence. He already knows all our needs, all our weaknesses, our hopes, and our fears. He is on our side, he is close to us, and he loves us. Prayer has been described as "spending time with God" and that is a very good description of it. Just as two lovers are happy to spend time together simply enjoying each other's company and presence so, too, in prayer we grow towards that kind of relationship with God.

That doesn't mean that we shouldn't speak to God in more basic ways like giving thanks, asking his help, and expressing our sorrow for sin and failure. But it is important that we don't let our prayer life stop there. Because it is only through developing our closeness and unity with God that we become more like Jesus Christ and so become a true reflection of his love in our world and in our relationships.

"The Spirit too comes to help us in our weakness. For when we cannot choose words in order to pray properly, the Spirit himself expresses our plea in a way that could never be put into words, and he who can see into all hearts knows what the Spirit means, and that the pleas of the saints expressed by the Spirit are according to the mind of God" (Romans 8:26-27).

In prayer we meet God. We learn to see the world and other people through his eyes. We begin, too, to see ourselves with his eyes and learn to understand what it means to be loved sincerely and unconditionally forever.

Jesus tells us about effective prayer:
"I say to you: Ask, and it will be given to you; search, and you will find; knock, and the door will be opened to you. For the one who asks always receives; the one who searches always finds; the one who knocks will always have the door opened to him. What father among you would hand his son a stone when he asked for bread? Or hand him a snake instead of a fish? Or hand him a scorpion if he asked for an egg? If you then, who are evil, know how to give your children what is good, how much more will the heavenly Father give the Holy Spirit to those who ask him!" (Luke 11:9-13)

The prayer of Jesus

In the great prayer of Christ following the Last Supper, which is recounted in John's gospel, Jesus takes his followers to the heart of the meaning of his life and his death which is to follow on the next day. In this prayer, Jesus shows us that prayer is at the center of his and of our relationship with God.

In this prayer Jesus glorifies his Father and gathers up all who follow him into that prayer. He prays for those who have heard his words and believed in him. He prays that in their unity with him, they may discover a unity among themselves, so that all may be one, united in Christ, and so united with his Father in heaven.

In this unity they will share in the redeeming work of Christ and in the suffering which he is to undergo. But in sharing that suffering they also share his glory. All who are faithful in unity with Christ will share the glory and joy of the resurrection. In all this, they are to be faithful not only to the words of Christ but also to his way of the cross, to his way of unconditional love for all men and women. Christ prays for his followers and will continue to pray for them; he will protect them and he will consecrate them to himself through his prayer always.

Prayer, then, unites us with Christ and with his Father so completely that the world will know that Christ was from God in our faithful reflection of his life and death.

First steps in prayer

Many of us find the road to prayer hard going. This is often because our approach to prayer is determined by a primitive view of God.

So many of us have not really listened to Jesus Christ telling us in his parables about the true nature of God. He speaks of the prodigal son; the host who invited everyone, even the most miserable beggar, to his table; and the woman caught in the act of sin. Yet we cling, in spite of everything, to the image of a God who is ever ready to avenge and punish us. Small wonder that we often find it a grim and nerve-racking experience to talk to such a God in prayer.

The apostles weren't afraid to ask Jesus to teach them how to pray. He knew their weakness and gently set them on the road to prayer. Many have traveled that same road since, and their experiences form part and parcel of the rich tradition of the Church.

It's impossible to outline here all the advice and guidance of so many men and women. But it is clear that there are certain steps which can help us develop a rich and authentic prayer life.

1. Prayer is a meeting

We cannot allow ourselves to forget this. Prayer is a meeting with God. It is not some magic formula for disciplining the mind. Neither is it a soothing way of escaping from the pressures and worries of life. First and foremost prayer is a meeting with our heavenly Father and if it is to be a real meeting, we must take the second step...

2. Be yourself

We've all heard of the sad clown who hides behind the smiling mask. All of us have a wardrobe full of masks, and we can use them as well as any quick-change artist.

The tragedy is that as long as we have our mask on nobody ever meets us. They meet the highly professional businessperson, the skilled worker, the loving mother, but they never see the insecure, anxious, sad clown that we really are. What a relief when we can reveal our true self to someone who loves us.

God loves you. God loves each one of us. It's easy to be ourselves with him. Once we try this, we find we have taken the second step in prayer. But if this meeting is to be a success, there is something else we must do...

3. Let God be God

It rarely strikes us how arrogant we are. We're like the child who told his mother he was about to draw God. "But no one knows what God looks like" he was told. "Not at the moment," he agreed, "but they will when I've finished."

We think we know and understand God. Somewhere in an old attic of our minds we store a picture of God and keep on bringing it out like some dog-eared photograph from the family album.

Yet there is a truth we cannot avoid. No man or woman can fully understand the Creator of all things. He is completely beyond our grasp or understanding. We have to learn to throw away all our preconceived notions and let God come to us as he really is, not as we would have him be. Then we are ready to take one more step forward...

4. Give God your worries

"Come to me all you who labor and are over-burdened and I will give you rest...." As long as we hang on to our worries we will have to carry a burden which is so unwieldy that it obscures our vision of God.

It's important that we take God at his word and give him all our worries. Once we start trusting God it's amazing how relieved we begin to feel. It's like taking a heavy backpack off our shoulders after a long gruelling walk.

Once this barrier has gone, we are ready to talk to God. We can use set prayers if we wish to or simply talk to him naturally if we are able to do so. Alternatively, we can simply sit in companionable silence with him. This leads us to a final step...

5. Listen

An old saying comes straight to the point: "God has given you two ears and one mouth that you may listen to him twice as much as you speak to him."

It's easy to ignore the obvious but a conversation is not only talking but listening. It is important for us to be silent and listen to our God speaking to us. More than that, we must let Jesus Christ speak through us. He will, if we give him the chance. And when he does, we will "with all the saints have strength to grasp the breadth and length, the height and depth; until knowing the love of God which is beyond all knowledge, you are filled with the utter fullness of God" (Ephesians 3:18-19).

Starting meditation

Some people find that meditation is the form of prayer, the way of communicating with God, which they feel helps them grow closer to God. A simple form of meditation revolves around a single word or a short phrase which is repeated steadily and rhythmically. The name "Jesus" has often been used in this way, either by itself or as part of a longer phrase. For example, during the season of Advent, a suitable phrase to use would be "Come, Lord Jesus."

The purpose of this phrase is twofold. First, it occupies the surface of the mind, aiding concentration, clearing away distractions, and helping to bring peace and stillness.

Second, it carries a power of its own. As one writer has put it, "The phrase, repeated and repeated until it is engraved on the tablets of the mind, has incredible motive power; it can heal, it can transfigure, it can transform."

Now here's an easy step-by-step guide to this form of meditation:

1. Find a place where you can be alone and undisturbed for the period of meditation—say between ten and twenty minutes.
2. Take up a firm but comfortable position—sitting up straight in a chair or cross-legged on the floor.
3. Lay your hands on your lap or on the arms of the chair. Close your eyes and relax.
4. Spend a few moments in silence, breathing gently and rhythmically.
5. Begin to say the phrase "Come, Lord Jesus" over and over again (in your mind rather than out loud). Say it slowly. You may find that after a while the words coincide with your breathing. This is a further aid to attentiveness, but don't try to force it.

The aim isn't to achieve anything or to experience anything. It's simply to be still and at peace, attentive to the presence of God in the depth of our hearts.

Jesus tells us how to pray

"In your prayers do not babble as the pagans do, for they think that by using many words they will make themselves heard. Do not be like them; your Father knows what you need before you ask him. So you should pray like this:

Our Father in heaven,
may your name be held holy,
your kingdom come,
your will be done,
on earth as in heaven.
Give us today our daily bread.
And forgive us our debts,
as we have forgiven those who are in debt to us.
And do not put us to the test,
but save us from the evil one.

Yes, if you forgive others their failings, your heavenly Father will forgive you yours; but if you do not forgive others, your Father will not forgive your failings either" (Matthew 6:7-15).

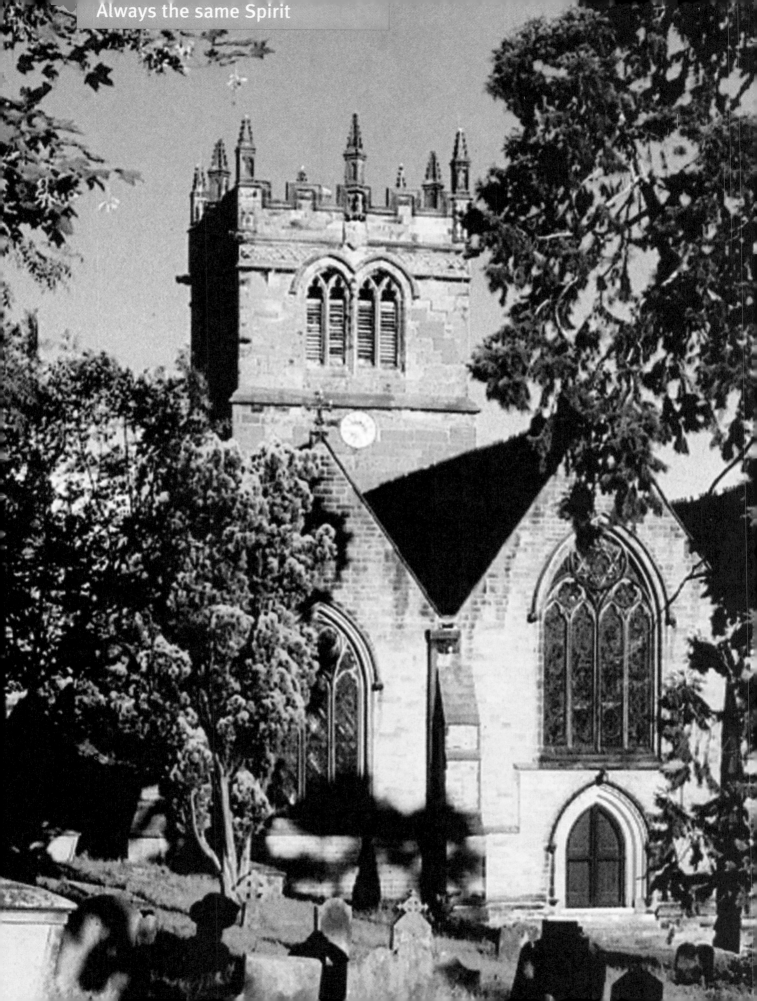

8. Always the same Spirit

Some time ago a parish priest wrote to every parishioner explaining that the annual cost of heating the church was several thousand dollars. He pointed out that, although it wasn't a large church, the roof was sixty feet high. To overcome the problem of costs the building was to be weather-proofed as much as possible, and he suggested that people dress more warmly, remembering that centuries ago churches weren't heated at all. "But," he continued, "the best way that parishioners can help is to bring a friend to church with them; for body heat is still our most precious natural energy resource."

The priest's suggestion was offered "tongue in cheek," but it was an obvious one. On average, the heat from three people is equivalent to a one kilowatt electric fire.

It is so easy to overlook the obvious. We can spend so much time building and repairing beautiful churches and constructing all kinds of efficient organizations for the running of the Church and end up giving no energy to the love—the warmth—that alone gives life to God's Church. A small congregation worshiping in a ramshackle building and willing to share their lives—even sharing their body heat—is far more certain to survive and grow than a mass of people sitting comfortably in a church kept cozy by central heating and so able to keep their distance from one another.

The beginning of the Church goes back to that day when the first followers of Jesus came together in a room to support one another. In the Gospel of John we are told that "the doors were closed in the room where the disciples were, for fear of the Jews." Then Jesus breathed on them and gave them his Spirit. In the Acts of the Apostles we have a more complete picture of what happened.

Again, it was after the resurrection of Jesus at the time when his followers were still unsure of what was happening.

"When Pentecost day came round, they had all met in one room, when suddenly they heard what sounded like a powerful wind from heaven, the noise of which filled the entire house in which they were sitting; and something appeared to them that seemed like tongues of fire; these separated and came to rest on the head of each of them. They were all filled with the Holy Spirit and began to speak foreign languages as the Spirit gave them the gift of speech" (Acts 2:1-4).

The writer of Acts then goes on to say how Peter, the leader of the apostles, told the people in Jerusalem about Jesus, how he had died and risen again, and how new life and the Spirit of Jesus was offered to all who acknowledged him. "That very day," we are told, "about three thousand were added to their number."

Today, it is estimated that there are over one billion followers of Jesus Christ in our world. Although growing larger by the day, the group of Christ's followers remains essentially unchanged. This assembly is known as the Church, from the Greek word *ekklesia*, meaning "an assembly called together."

The Church, then, is not a building. It's a gathering of people. And although each one of us is unique, we are held together by the Spirit of Jesus who lives within each one of us, drawing us closer to God and to one another and who enables us to acknowledge Jesus as our Lord.

When Jesus spoke about the future of his followers he painted certain characteristics which, today, are summarized in the Creed which we say at Mass. We profess our belief in "one, holy, catholic, and apostolic Church." It will be helpful to look at each of these in turn.

The Church is one

This means that we are united in the life of God. Jesus spoke of himself as a vine: "I am the vine, you are the branches. Whoever remains in me, with me in him, bears fruit in plenty; for cut off from me you can do nothing." The Spirit of God who unites us is like the sap in the vine: normally we can't see it yet it gives life. And the proof that we are alive is that we bear fruit which refreshes and nourishes the world in which we live.

The Church is holy

Jesus, the Son of God, shared his life with us wholly. And he promised that he would continue to do so. "If anyone loves me," he says, "he will keep my word and my Father will love him, and we shall come to him and make our home with him." Jesus is "at home" with us. Our lives can, and so often do, bring others to God.

The Church is catholic

This means that the Church embraces all peoples in every age. The final command of Jesus was to "go and make disciples of all nations and baptize them in the name of the Father and of the Son and of the Holy Spirit." The Church, then, is not an exclusive club for those we happen to regard as suitable. It is for everyone.

The Church is apostolic

It is God who calls us together as a Church. But we remain human beings. The Church is formed by God as an organization built upon human beings and, in particular, on the apostles and their successors, the bishops. "You are Peter," Jesus said to his chief apostle, "and on this rock I will build my Church." The Bishop of Rome remains the successor of Saint Peter. Like Peter, they are not always a solid rock yet it is so often in human weakness that the power of God becomes most evident.

The Church is people

Jesus certainly had to deal with a great deal of weakness from his own closest followers. One of the apostles, Philip, said to Jesus on the night before he died, "Lord, let us see the Father and then we shall be satisfied." It was with some exasperation that Jesus replied: "To have seen me is to have seen the Father." A few years later Saint Paul said essentially the same thing. He described Jesus as "the image of the unseen God" (Colossians 1:15) and "the revelation of a mystery kept secret for endless ages" (Romans 16:25).

These words, "secret" and "mystery," have very similar meanings and they give us the word "sacrament." (The word "sacrament" comes from the Latin word "*sacramentum*" which in turn comes from the Greek word for "mystery.") Both Jesus and Paul were emphasizing the same truth: if we want to see what God is like then look at Jesus himself and hear what he says and see what he does. And today, now that Jesus has returned to his Father, if we want to see what Jesus is like we are to look at his Church and hear what the Church says and see what it does. Sometimes we refer to Jesus as the "sacrament" of God; and we refer to the Church as the "sacrament of Jesus Christ." "From the side of Christ," the Church tells us, "came forth the wondrous sacrament of the whole Church."

It is impossible to overemphasize the closeness between Jesus Christ and the Church. The very first act of Jesus after his resurrection was to breathe on the apostles in the small room where they had gathered together for comfort and give them his Holy Spirit. But Jesus looked beyond that room until the end of time and prayed to his Father that all people would come together and forgive one another so that "they may all be one." "Father," he prayed, "may they be one in us, as you are in me and I am in you, so that the world may believe it was you who sent me."

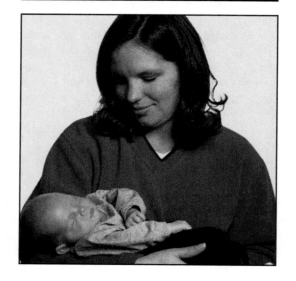

The Church, then, is the people who come together as one people to share in the goodness of God and to celebrate it. Each time we assemble we gather in the warmth of God's love. The little room in which Jesus first appeared has been enlarged to take in the whole world and every age. And so the Church describes herself as "a people brought into unity from the unity of the Father, the Son, and the Holy Spirit" (Vatican II).

The Trinity

The life of God—the life of the Father, the Son, and the Holy Spirit—is at the heart of the Church's existence and teaching. Jesus confirmed our belief that God is not unmoved or unconcerned by humankind and that he loves us deeply. Jesus Christ told us that he was wholly one with the Father and that he sends his Holy Spirit to unite us with God.

We refer to the doctrine of the Holy Trinity as a "mystery." The "mystery" of the Trinity does not primarily have to do with how the one God exists in three Persons. The "mystery" of the Trinity is primarily about relationships—the perfect relationship between the Father, the Son, and the Holy Spirit.

This is difficult to understand because we're not very good at relationships. We're better at using our intellect and, over the centuries, our fund of knowledge has increased dramatically. At the same time, however, our ability to enter into happy relationships hasn't improved at all. The first experience of man and woman was a sense of loneliness and isolation. Such loneliness continues to cut across wealth or power or status.

It may be obvious, but it is a truth worth repeating, nonetheless, that God did not involve himself with humankind because he was lonely and bored. The Son, Jesus, didn't come among us for a "chat" as we might go to our neighbor for a cup of coffee. For the Father, the Son, and the Holy Spirit enjoy a perfect relationship. They do not suffer loneliness. Their happiness and the love between them is perfect and complete. And we say that the relationship among them is a great mystery, not because it is a truth about which we can know nothing, but because it is a truth about which we can never know everything. Our relationship with God can never be complete in this life because we're not very good at relationships. And so the mystery of the Trinity remains a constant challenge to us, beyond our thoughts and words.

There are certain truths about the Trinity that we can learn, however. A good relationship is always based on loving—on giving. And each Person of the Trinity has been given to us in a particular way.

We recognize the Father in particular as the origin of creation and of the re-creation. "God loved the world so much," Jesus tells us "that he gave his only Son."

And the Son, Jesus, is the Person of the Trinity who united himself with human flesh in order to reveal God's love. The penalty he paid was a painful death because the world wasn't interested. He gave himself to us in flesh and blood, just as he continues to give himself, under the form of bread and wine, in the Eucharist.

And the Holy Spirit, finally, is the third Person of the Trinity who comes into the world every day to draw humankind into the love of God. He is the love of God who draws us to the Father and to one another. Jesus called him the "Comforter." The Holy Spirit is usually regarded as the expression of the mutual love between Father and Son: similarly he is the bond of love between the Father and humankind. When he comes to us he enables us to cry out, "Abba, Father," which is the cry of the child entering into a perfect relationship with the heavenly Father.

To begin to understand these relationships within the Trinity and to enter into their mystery is more than the work of a lifetime; it is the work of eternity. For we are not talking about a mathematical formula or a scientific analysis in which, at the end of our search for a solution or answer, we can experience the joy of crying out: "I've solved it" or "I've discovered it." We are talking about relationships. And in a relationship there is always room for growth.

As our relationship with God does grow we begin to overcome our loneliness. We begin to enter into a communion far more profound than a purely human community. We enter into the life of the Father, the Son, and the Holy Spirit.

The Holiness of the Church?

The Church tends to get bad press these days—not only from people outside but also from critics within her own ranks, particularly among younger members. Critics often concentrate on the Church as an institution, and institutions, they say, are cold, heartless things, ever ready to stamp on anyone who steps out of line. But it's not only the institution that comes in for criticism. Attention is also drawn to the many Catholics who clearly fail to live up to their Christian ideals.

The Church accepts the failure of her members

Criticisms of the failures of those human beings who make up the Church are fully justified. The Church herself freely acknowledges that she is far from perfect, "The Church is well aware that some of her members, clerical and lay, have in the course of centuries turned out to be unfaithful to the Spirit of God. In our times too she does not overlook the gulf between the message she brings and the human failings of those to whom the Gospel has been entrusted" (Vatican II).

Yet, while acknowledging that the Church has many faults and failings, we also maintain that the Church is "holy." Isn't that something of a contradiction? We say that the Church is holy but in fact the Church doesn't really look all that holy all the time.

How can this be resolved? First of all by realizing that when we speak of the holiness of the Church we are not speaking primarily of the holiness of its members but of the holiness of Jesus Christ. Through the Church, the holiness of Jesus Christ becomes present among men and women.

That holiness is a gift, freely given through the power of the Holy Spirit who dwells in the hearts of all Christians. So, every Christian carries within him or her the holiness of Christ.

The holiness of Christ is offered to all in the Church

Clearly this holiness ought to be reflected in the life of each individual Christian; it ought to be expressed in a life of goodness, a life of love and service modeled on Jesus himself. Some Christians do achieve this; they are the saints of the Church—canonized and uncanonized. But for most of us it's a different story. We often fail to live up to the gift we have been given; we ignore or reject the murmur of the Holy Spirit within us.

It is here that we see again the amazing extent of God's love. In spite of our failure, in spite of our faithlessness and sinfulness, God, through his Spirit, continues to give himself to us. He's ready to welcome us again and again, to make us holy in spite of ourselves and our foolishness.

This should not surprise us. For while Jesus was on earth he mixed freely with sinners and the outcasts of society. In doing so he showed us what true holiness is; not judgment and condemnation, but redeeming love.

The Church continues the redeeming work of Jesus. The Church must, therefore, draw sinners to her and offer them—through the proclamation of the Gospel and the celebration of the sacraments—the holiness of Christ. This the Church continues to do, no matter how much Christ's holiness may be obscured by the failure and sinfulness of individual members.

Are there other churches?

There can only be one Church. It would be absurd to believe that Jesus, the Son of God, should come among us with the intention of building up several communities of his followers, each going its separate way.

It is clear from the words of Jesus that he intended his followers to be at one with one another. "Father," he prayed, "may they all be one. May they be one in us as you are in me and I am in you, so that the world may believe it was you who sent me."

In Christ's Church there are two elements to this oneness. First, there is the oneness we can see. This is the unity which is visible when, for example, Christians come together for prayer, worship, and to build up the world into a better place.

The second element to the oneness of Christ's followers is what we can't see. It is the life of God—the Holy Spirit—who dwells within each person who lives according to his or her conscience, which is the voice of God speaking from within. The Holy Spirit is the love of God who comes as a gift to every human being. As Pope John Paul II has reminded us, "With each person, without any exception whatever, Christ is in a way united, even when we are unaware of it."

In the ideal world, the visible and invisible elements would be in perfect harmony. The Spirit of God, active in so many people, would create a wonderful unity. And so at the end of Mass, for example, we are invited to "go in peace to love and serve the Lord." This is a reminder that the oneness we have celebrated in our coming together for worship is a oneness which should be seen in our common objective of creating a happier world. Such harmony is the fulfillment of the kingdom of God.

However, we don't live in the ideal world—at least, not yet! It is the teaching of the Catholic Church that the visible elements of Christ's Church are most clearly to be found in the Catholic Church. We believe that unity of worship and purpose is centered on the Mass, the supreme celebration of Christ's presence. This unity and purpose are presided over by the bishops, chief of whom is the Bishop of Rome. To be separated from the pope is to be removed from the visible center of unity of Christ's Church.

The Catholic Church can make no claim to a monopoly of the invisible life of the Church—the life of the Holy Spirit of God. This life of God comes from the love of God made visible in Jesus Christ who established his Church to make such love known until the end of time. It is obvious, however, that many people share in this life who are not visibly united to the Catholic Church, and the proof of this is that so many people enjoy the gifts of the Spirit—such gifts as love, joy, peace, patience, kindness, goodness, trustfulness, gentleness, and self-control (Galatians 5:22). So many people, too, are able to call God their "Father" and recognize his goodness.

There is one Church, then, but people are united with the one Church in different ways. Here are some of the principal ways:

1 Those who belong to the Roman Catholic Church share in the visible life of Christ's Church most clearly. It might be added that this doesn't always make Catholics better people—too often, quite the reverse. Nor is it a reason for self-congratulation. Rather, the Church is a gift given to many who are to work for the clear, visible unity of all men and women throughout the world.

2 Those who belong to other Christian communities share in the invisible life of the Church—the life of the Holy Spirit—and in many of her visible signs of unity also. For example, they share in the sacrament of baptism and in the written word of God. Many such Christians are good and holy people—far better than some Roman Catholics. Yet their separation from the visible source of unity is a reminder of failures in the past and an incentive to work for closer unity today.

3 Those who do not belong to any Christian community do not share in the visible life of the Church but nonetheless share in her invisible life—the life of God. These are people who "seek God with a sincere heart and try in their actions to do his will as they know it through the dictates of their conscience" (Vatican II). The fact that such people do not belong visibly to the life of the Church until the kingdom of God is fully established is a reminder to Catholics that we have a great deal to do in continuing Christ's own desire that we work for the unity of all.

Origin of sacraments

When Jesus died on the cross, his disciples were confused, frightened, and unsure of their future. In the days following his resurrection, they gathered together for mutual support and to try to make sense of what was happening.

As they gathered together, Jesus came among them. He was different from the Jesus they were familiar with and yet they recognized him and knew him in his words and in his actions.

In listening to his words they began to understand more fully who he was and what his message meant. His vision and his teaching about life, which he had shared with them when he was with them before his crucifixion, was now in sharp focus. As they listened to his words they recognized him as the Son of God; they knew he was indeed the Christ.

In witnessing his actions in the resurrection, in the breaking of bread, and in the sharing of himself, they came to share the reality of his faith, his unity with his heavenly Father, and an understanding of his responsibility and love for all men and women.

The disciples experienced the action and the power of the Holy Spirit in and through this unity with Jesus Christ and with one another. As a result of this they gained in confidence and courage to move out from that frightened, nervous group, hiding away in a "safe" meeting place. They moved out into the world to share in turn what they had received; mutual support, the word of God, and the experience of the Spirit of Jesus in transforming and renewing life.

This pattern has remained essentially the same in the life and work of the Body of Christ—the Church—from the earliest days until now.

At the heart of the life of the Church are the sacraments which constantly renew and reconcile the Church and its believers to God. And the celebration of every sacrament follows the original pattern experienced by that very first community of believers following the resurrection:

- Christ's followers gather together as a community.

- This community listens to the word of God and they break bread.

- The community share the experience of God's action.

- They depart to serve others and bring them the Good News.

It is clear from this pattern that being a follower of Christ is not simply a private arrangement between God and the individual. The opposite is true. Being a follower of Christ means being part of a community, part of the Body of Christ here on earth, today. In becoming part of that Body we don't lose our own individuality; rather we become more fully ourselves because we are accepted as free to be what God has created us to be. And we accept others on the same basis because in our baptism we are united in God and in his love and care for every other person.

It is only when we are afraid to show our weaknesses, afraid of what others may do to us, or afraid of being ignored that we move into the false security of isolation.

Jesus came to free every person from such isolation. He came to make us truly free and in his life he showed us the reality of what being human really meant. Being truly human means being Christlike. Anything which prevents that makes us less than a fully human being.

Holy oils

For the people of God in the Old Testament, oil had a significant role. Oil is burned to give heat and light, and is used for cooking as well. On a more intimate level, oil penetrates deeply into the body giving strength, health, suppleness, and beauty. It's not surprising, then, that to be anointed with oil was a sign of rejoicing and respect. In the Old Testament, too, we read of anointings taking place as part of the rites of consecration. The outward significance of these anointings were that the anointed one had been chosen by God to be his sign to the people. A king so anointed became a sharer in the Spirit of God.

"Christ" means "anointed one" for Jesus was given a special work to do. He suffered and rose again in order to unite us to his heavenly Father. A Christian, as a reflection of Christ, also has special work to do in living as a member of Christ's Body, the Church, and in revealing Christ to other men and women. For this reason, "anointing" with oil plays a significant part in our celebration of the sacraments as a sign of being an "anointed one."

Every Holy Thursday the bishop of each diocese blesses the oils which are to be used for anointing throughout his diocese during the year ahead. These oils are then distributed to priests for use in their celebration of the sacraments with their local Christian community.

Three oils are blessed:

- **Oil of Catechumens** or Oil of Baptism is used for anointing new members of the Christian community. The basis of this oil is olive oil.

- **Oil of Chrism** is used as a sign of sealing with the gifts of the Holy Spirit and is used when a profession of faith is made at baptism, at confirmation, and at the ordination of priests. This oil is a sweet-smelling oil and is based on a mixture of olive oil and balsam.

- **Oil of the Sick** is used to anoint those who are sick and those who are dying. This oil is a sign of healing of body, mind, and soul. The basis of this oil is olive oil.

9. The Creative Spirit
The sacrament of baptism

Baptism is our proof and our confirmation of our **Creative God:** a God who in his love and longing to be one with us reaches out and invites us to join with him in being creative. Physically, he enables us to procreate; to bear new life as a continual development and sign of human unity. Spiritually, too, he enables us to procreate, to bear new life in faith as a result of our unity in faith with him and with one another.

Baptism is our beginning not our arrival

Our baptism is simply the beginning of our life of faith. The beginning of getting to know and understand what being loved by God means. Baptism is God's token to us of his great love—it's a love token. In all sacraments faith carries us forward to the sacrament, but when we are baptized as babies it is the faith of our parents which carries us to the sacrament. It follows then that to fulfill the true meaning of the sacrament and to achieve the authenticity of the sign of baptism, there must be continuing teaching and example of living faith. If this doesn't happen, although the sacrament is valid, the significance of it is prevented from having its full effect. It's easy to see, then, that what happens after baptism is vitally important if we are to experience the fulfillment of the promise of this fundamental sacrament.

What difference does baptism make?

At baptism, we join God's family and become a baby Christian. As with most things in life, being baptized won't necessarily make much difference to us unless there is further input. Being baptized is the beginning of something, it is not an isolated event or a magic moment which acts like a good-luck charm for life. Jesus Christ asks us to baptize in his name so that parents, godparents, and God can work together in a creative partnership throughout the crucial years ahead as we grow to maturity.

For the first nine months of life a baby lives in the womb totally dependent on its mother for life and nourishment. After birth a baby continues to be dependent on its mother and the immediate family for continuing care for many years until he or she is mature enough to live as an adult.

A baby only grows and will only continue growing as long as the care, protection, and guidance needed to reach successful maturity continues to be given. In the same way a "baby" Christian will only grow and continue to grow as a Christian if there is support, example, and teaching throughout childhood and adolescence. By bringing their child to be baptized, parents are giving a sign to the world that they and God are indeed partners working together for the complete development of their child—body and soul. As with other aspects of growing up, if support and encouragement are not given or are withdrawn too early, permanent immaturity is the result. It's not always too difficult to spot that among ourselves as Christians.

Our faith makes a creative difference

It's very difficult to be a member of a family if you never have any contact with other members of the family. And it's very unreasonable to expect anyone to bring up a child as a Christian if they're not trying to live as Christians themselves. For these reasons the Church is more concerned than ever today that parents who ask for their child to be baptized also understand what is involved and understand what their commitment and responsibilities will be concerning the growing faith of their child. It's no good expecting anyone to bring up a child as a Catholic when neither parent is practicing their faith.

Often parents ask for baptism for their baby because they think it's a nice celebration for the family, or grandparents say that the baby must be baptized. It may be that they think of baptism as a special kind of blessing which will safeguard the child. All these reasons are very understandable but they are not the real purpose for seeking baptism.

As we have seen, in baptism, it is the faith of the parents which brings the baby to church. Babies are baptized because, as children of believing and practicing Christians, they have been born and are living within the Christian community. Baptism brings them into this family of God. Being part of a family means growing up in the ways of that family. It means belonging, learning, sharing, in a certain way of life. That is the meaning of baptism; it's a sign of the beginning of life as a Christian.

What is the point of baptizing a baby if he or she will not be able to grow and develop within the family of God? If parents are not practicing their faith they cannot be expected to be able or willing to pass it on to their child. And it is unfair and unreasonable to tie any child to a Church and way of life to which they will have no real attachment other than being bound by certain church laws as an adult. Our faith is a creative relationship with God, not a set of rules. The faith of parents and godparents, then, is crucial in baptism.

The creativity of God—baptism is our invitation

God created us with great love. He wanted us to exist, he wanted us to be part of his creative life. Since our baptism, our beginning of life in and with Christ, we may have lost sight of, or perhaps forgotten, God's creativity in our life. Whatever has happened to us, whatever the quality of our relationships with the Church and with other Christians, God continues to invite us to share in his creativity.

What is baptism?

Baptism means "plunging." Jesus was baptized in the river Jordan by John. The sign of the Holy Spirit was seen, and the Father's voice was heard, "This is my Son, the Beloved; my favor rests on him" (Matthew 3:17).

Jesus called his death and resurrection a "baptism." To his apostles he said, "Are you willing to be baptized with the baptism with which I must be baptized?" In this baptism Jesus was "plunged" into death, but the Father raised him up by giving him the Holy Spirit.

Baptism is the sign instituted by Jesus to unite us with his own baptism. What happened at Jesus' death and resurrection is what happens at baptism, so that Saint Paul could write, "When we were baptized in Christ Jesus we were baptized in his death; in other words, when we were baptized we went into the tomb with him and joined him in death, so that as Christ was raised from the dead by the Father's glory, we too might live a new life" (Romans 6:3-4).

Baptism is a sign of salvation because it is the sacrament introduced by Jesus to make us part of his Body, the Church. Jesus told Nicodemus, "I tell you most solemnly, unless a man is born of water and the Spirit, he cannot enter the kingdom of God" (John 3:5).

Water

This liquid is for cleansing and is a sign that our sins are washed away. Baptism cleanses us from original sin with which we are all born and, in the baptism of adults, of every sin committed prior to baptism.

Water is also a sign of new life. The newly baptized is given the new life of the Holy Spirit which unites the person in the life of the Trinity. We call this new life "sanctifying grace."

The Christian name given at the baptism is a symbol of the truth that the newly baptized person belongs to Christ and is made like him.

What are the effects of baptism?

Baptism gives us the character of Christ. This is like the impression made by a parent on their child; it is permanent and irrevocable. Augustine compared the baptismal character to the mark or seal tattooed on a soldier to show who was his lord. When the sacrament is celebrated validly, the baptismal character is always given. Therefore, this sacrament can never be repeated. Because baptism confers the character of Christ, it gives the one who is baptized a share in Christ's priesthood and the power therefore to worship. This is the reason why a person must be baptized before being able to celebrate any other sacraments.

Godparents

In the earliest days of the Church, the sponsors at the baptism of a child were the parents. But since most of the baptisms in those days were of older candidates, this was often not possible. Many parents of converts could not or would not stand as sponsors. Slaves were without their parents, and many younger children had been abandoned by their parents and had to be taken in by Christian communities. Very often sponsors at these baptisms were deacons or deaconesses. Only one sponsor was required; in the case of adults, the person had to be of the same sex as the candidate. These sponsors were called "spiritual parents" and their duty was to give instruction both before and after baptism and to be a guardian of the spiritual life of the baptized person. This is the origin of the term "godparent."

Today, the role of godparents is secondary to that of the parents in the case of infant baptism. If necessary, godparents should be ready to help in the spiritual education of their godchild. It's important that a godparent is sufficiently mature (usually over sixteen), already initiated as a Christian (by baptism, confirmation, and the Eucharist), and a member of the Catholic Church.

Today, a parent cannot be godparent to his or her own child.

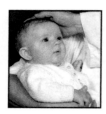 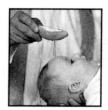 

What happens at baptism?

- Those who are to be baptized, their families and friends, and the community of Christians, gather together to celebrate this sign of God's life in the world.

- Words of welcome are exchanged. The names that have been chosen for baptism are announced and all present are united in the opening prayers.

- Everyone present listens to the word of God read from the Scriptures.

- Prayers are offered for those who are to receive the sacrament, for their families, friends, and all who are present.

- To prepare for baptism the candidate is anointed with Oil of Baptism as a sign of Christ's strengthening power in overcoming evil.

- All present renew their own baptismal vows.

- The baptism takes place. The minister pours the baptismal water over the forehead three times as he says the words of baptism.

- The newly baptized are then anointed with Oil of Chrism as a sign of being sealed with the gifts of the Holy Spirit. Like Christ the one baptized is now an "anointed one."

- As a sign of being a new creation clothed in Christ, the one who has been baptized is now clothed in a white garment.

- A candle lit from the Easter candle is presented as a sign of the light of Christ now present in the newly baptized life.

- Final prayers are said and a blessing is given that all present may love and serve the Lord in peace and goodwill.

The Baptism of Adults

A baby is brought to baptism in the Church by the faith of his or her parents. This is clearly not so for adults who, after hearing about Jesus Christ, are moved by the Holy Spirit within them to consciously and freely seek baptism.

The growth of the Church in the first centuries came very largely through the baptism of adults. In more recent years the Church has returned to many of the ceremonies of those first centuries for welcoming people who seek baptism into the Church. The whole period of deepening conversion and the ceremonies that accompany it have been brought together in what the Church calls the Rite of Christian Initiation of Adults, or RCIA.

The RCIA is a reminder of a truth that has always been recognized by the Christian community: to be a Christian it isn't enough to walk off the street and into a church and ask a priest for baptism. There is no such thing as an "overnight conversion." Growth in faith, rather, is a gradual process and this is as true for an adult seeking baptism as it is for someone baptized as a baby who then grows into the faith as he or she matures into childhood, adolescence, and adulthood. It is this usually gradual growth in faith which frequently leads the Christian life to be referred to as a "journey" or "pilgrimage." For in every Christian's growth in faith there are periods of rapid movement but also times when we hardly know where we are going; there are moments of excitement but also situations where we experience an uphill struggle. And so all the steps of the RCIA may take a year or two or even more. The steps mark important moments of growth in the knowledge and love of

God which apply to people seeking baptism but which can be applied equally to all Christians who seek to mature in faith.

Even a simple chart of these rites of the RCIA which mark entry of an adult into the Church can appear rather complicated and daunting. Most dioceses and parishes adapt the ceremonies to their own particular circumstances. It is useful, however, to chart the rites in a way which provides an overall picture of the RCIA process.

OUTLINE FOR CHRISTIAN INITIATION OF ADULTS The initiation of adults into the Catholic Church may be divided into three principal steps, each step being preceded and followed by a period of maturing in faith.

FIRST STEP
Acceptance into the order of catechumens

First public declaration of intention to become a member of the Church.

SECOND STEP
Election or enrollment of names

Usually celebrated on the First Sunday of Lent when the Church formally accepts candidates for entry into the Church and enrolls their names in the book kept for that purpose.

THIRD STEP
Celebration of sacraments of initiation

that is, baptism, confirmation, and Eucharist—usually at the Easter Vigil.

Period of Post-Baptismal Instruction (Mystagogy)

usually takes place during the Easter season, when the newly baptized are more fully drawn into the Christian community, especially through the Sunday Eucharist, for the deepening of commitment of all God's faithful.

Period of Purification and Enlightenment

usually takes place during the season of Lent. It is a time of reflection centered on conversion. It includes the scrutinies and presentations of the Creed and the Lord's Prayer.

Period of Catechumenate

is of no fixed duration. In this period the candidate's faith is nurtured, and instruction is received in the mysteries of faith and the teachings of the Catholic Church. It includes celebrations of the word of God and blessings.

Period of Evangelization

is of no fixed duration. It is the period when the candidate is introduced to the Gospel and experiences the beginnings of faith.

Committed Catholics are usually very busy people. They are involved in lots of things; they have a lot to do. Committed Catholics seem to be involved in so many activities and organizations; they support parish activities, they support the schools, they support moral and civil rights organizations. They are also involved in liturgy, catechetics, and fund-raising, from rummage sales to full-blown festivals and bazaars. It would be easy for an onlooker to think that to be a "real" Catholic means you have to have an extra shot of energy and drive for all worthy causes.

Unfortunately, many people's image of the sacrament of confirmation reinforces this idea. All too often confirmation is seen as the sacrament of Christian action or the sacrament of becoming a "Soldier of Christ." All of these ideas and images can be very misleading.

Confirmation celebrates the presence of the Holy Spirit within us

Our confirmation is, in fact, a continuance of what has begun at our baptism; a continuance of the developing awareness and reality of faith and the presence of the Holy Spirit in our lives. At our baptism, faith was conceived; we became part of Christ's Body; part of his Church. The Holy Spirit ensures that we are a brother or sister of Christ. Our confirmation is the gentle unfolding of what our baptism means.

When we celebrate confirmation, we celebrate the fact that we are being transformed, and that transformation will continue to take place from the day we are confirmed until we are completely one with God. We are on a journey to wholeness, peace, and perfecting love. We can celebrate that. Our heavenly Father celebrates with us because we are responding to his invitation to a life of love and reconciliation. We have said "yes" to his invitation to be part of the visible, living, breathing, Spirit-filled Body of Christ. It is only through the action and lives of Christians that the Holy Spirit, through faith and the sacraments, can show what the Church is truly called to be; the living Body of Christ. And this must be at the heart of any other activity we undertake.

The gifts of the Holy Spirit

There is an ancient tradition in the Church of speaking about the seven gifts of the Holy Spirit. The custom can be traced to Isaiah 11:1-3, and it sets down the following gifts:

- **Knowledge:** The gift of knowing the truth; knowing the Father and Jesus the Savior whom he sent among us.
- **Wisdom:** The power to see all things as God sees them.
- **Understanding:** The gift of understanding God's revelation.
- **Counsel:** The gift of helping us to see just what we should do in a difficult situation.
- **Fortitude:** The power to carry through joyfully what we know to be right.
- **Piety:** The gift that leads us to feel for God the love that a child feels for a loving parent and enables us to see all others as our brothers and sisters.
- **Fear of the Lord:** The gift that enables us to be willing to respond to the impulses of the Holy Spirit and gives us a fear of being separated from God.

It's important to remember, though, that *being* a Christian is the first gift of the Holy Spirit, and that each person has special gifts which the Holy Spirit uses for the good of the whole Church.

10. The Living Spirit
The sacrament of confirmation

What is confirmation?

During the life of Jesus and after his death and resurrection his followers grew to know and love him. They began to see in his teaching an answer to the questions and problems they encountered in their lives. Once they had witnessed his resurrection, they became completely convinced that they wanted to remain his followers for the rest of their lives. Just before his ascension, Jesus told them to spread the message of the Good News he had brought to them to the whole world. He then promised that he would be with them always (Matthew 28:20). The significance of this promise failed to register with them until the first Pentecost, the day when the disciples were filled with the Holy Spirit. Then, suddenly, they had the courage to speak out, strength to begin building a Christian community, and an amazing power to convince others of the truth of what they said about Jesus.

It is this strength, courage, and power which is the Spirit of Christ. Jesus was true to his word, he hadn't left them, his Spirit came into their hearts, permanently. This same Spirit enters our lives in this active way at our confirmation.

From the earliest days of the Church the gift of the Holy Spirit has been linked to baptism. In the Acts of the Apostles we read how Philip, the deacon, made converts in Samaria and baptized them. The apostles then sent Peter and John to the converts. On arrival "they prayed for them that they might receive the Holy Spirit for as yet he had not come upon any of them because they had only been baptized in the name of the Lord Jesus. Then they laid their hands on them and they received the Holy Spirit" (Acts 8:14-17).

Later, when Paul came to Ephesus, he found "disciples... who had not even heard that there is a Holy Spirit." They had received only John's baptism. When they heard of Christ, "they were baptized in the name of the Lord Jesus; and when Paul laid his hands on them, the Holy Spirit came upon them, and they began to speak in tongues and prophesy" (Acts 19:1-6).

In each case baptism was followed by the laying on of hands. Just as Jesus had invited his followers to join him, it was only after they had received the Holy Spirit that they were able to go out and pass on the Good News about the kind of life Jesus had revealed to them. So it is with us; we receive the invitation and accept it at baptism. This is followed by "the laying on of hands" at confirmation which inspires us to preach the Gospel.

The Spirit of Life

A once-popular children's party game—for parents as well as children—was Dead Lions. It's especially useful when things seem to be getting out of hand. Everyone lies flat on the floor pretending to be dead, there must not even be a flicker of life. Meanwhile, the person who is "it" tries to spot any movement, laughter, or breathing. The great advantage is that it provides about three minutes of peace! For those who are supposed to be "dead" its disadvantage is that it is almost impossible to lie "dead" still. Suddenly, we become aware that even our breathing, usually unnoticed, is ruining our chances of staying in the game.

Breathing is like that—we forget about it most of the time but at every key moment in life we watch anxiously for it. At birth, however well the baby looks, however smooth the delivery, we dare not relax until the first breath is drawn. And then, as we watch life slip away, we wait with bated breath ourselves for the final breath; and when there is no more breathing we cannot believe the silence.

In confirmation we receive the Holy Spirit. The Holy Spirit is the breath—the life—of God. And it is given to us. We share the life of God.

And in this breathing of God's life into our own souls we are given the gift of tongues just as the apostles were given it. For in the Holy Spirit we receive God's love which gives us the power to love as God loves. And love is a common language to all people. Love unites: we can speak to all men and women in all nations in this universal language which says, "You matter...you are of infinite value."

Much of the time as Christians we play Dead Lions with our heavenly Father. We just don't move as Christians, we fail to reveal the gift given to us in confirmation; we fail to breathe in the life of the Spirit. Yet we know that to give up breathing altogether is certain death. In every effort we make, no matter how small, to follow Christ, we are already responding to the breath of the Holy Spirit—the language of love. And that language of love, received at our baptism and confirmation, is the breath of eternal life which God continues to share with all who choose to follow the way revealed to us by Jesus Christ.

"The gift of the Holy Spirit closes the last gap between the life of God and ours... When we allow the love of God to move in us, we can no longer distinguish ours and his; he becomes us, he lives in us. It is the first fruit of the Holy Spirit, the beginning of our being made divine" (*Austin Farrer*).

What happens at confirmation?

- Those to be confirmed, their families, friends, and the community of Christians, gather together to celebrate this sign of God's life in the world.

- Words of welcome are exchanged and all present are united in the opening prayers.

- Everyone listens to the word of God which is read from the Scriptures.

- All Christians present renew their own baptismal vows.

- A prayer is offered, calling on the power of the Holy Spirit, and the bishop then lays his hands on the head of each candidate.

- The sponsors may each present their candidate to the bishop giving their candidate's chosen confirmation name.

- Each candidate is anointed by the bishop with Oil of Chrism calling them by their chosen name to be sealed with the gifts of the Holy Spirit.

- Prayers are then offered for all present, for the Church, and for all men and women.

- The celebration of the Eucharist follows.

Living the Christian life

Being a Christian means that "making a fresh start" is always possible. The Holy Spirit guiding us and prompting us gives us confidence and courage to face our failures and to try again to follow Christ. When Christ appeared to his followers after his resurrection his first words were "Peace be with you." Later, he promised to send the gift of the Holy Spirit to them to make that "peace" possible. There are five key points to living as a Christian:

1. **Accept change:** Jesus said that "unless you change and become as little children you cannot enter the kingdom of heaven." Most of us prefer a cozy existence in which we are disturbed and bothered as little as possible. And we prefer it when God leaves us alone. If we are going to enjoy new life then we have to leave that old life behind. It means accepting a God who enters into our lives totally. And so we have to want to follow Christ perfectly and experience the happiness and peace which only he brings. If we really want to become a Christian and are prepared to pay the price for it and have our life upset as a result then we have made the first step on the way to our own resurrection.

2. **Accept your own failings:** Sins and failures are not, in themselves, a barrier to God. The barrier is a stubborn heart and will in which we say to God, "keep away." Jesus didn't keep away from the company of sinners but only from the proud. The life and work of Jesus are full of his consolation for those who have fallen and lie in defeat. Our God is the God of those who fail. This doesn't mean that he loves failures more than others, but simply that he helps them more because he sees and understands their needs. Saint Paul once made the extraordinary statement: "If I am to boast, then let me boast of my own feebleness." Paul's realization of his own weakness was the moment of truth in his own spiritual struggle; and the Lord reassured him, "My power is at its best in weakness." Our consciousness of weakness gives God room to work. Pride alone makes God powerless.

3. **Accept the failings of others:** This means realizing first that others are like ourselves; and second, that they have a right to our forgiveness just as God forgives us. The alternative is far more damaging to us than to them. Our refusal to forgive means taking on the burden of hate. As Martin Luther King, Jr., wrote, "I've seen too much hate to hate myself...and every time I see it, I say to myself, hate is too great a burden to bear...." One of the first conditions of prayer is a forgiving heart. Clara Barton, founder of the American Red Cross, never held a grudge. Once a friend reminded her of something cruel that had been done to her. "Don't you remember the wrong that was done to you?" the friend asked. "No," Clara replied, "I distinctly remember forgetting that."

4. **Keep an eye on God:** Saint Francis de Sales tells us we are always to be like very small children going for a walk along a country lane. They cling with one hand to their loving parent while they gather blackberries with the other. If we ask our heavenly Father to hold us in his arms all the time we will remain as babies. But if we hold on to him with one hand while we gather and handle the things of this world with the other, we are free to turn to him from time to time to see if he is pleased with what we are doing. To let go of our heavenly Father altogether on the pretext of gathering more will result in our stumbling. Prayer is the way of keeping our attention fixed on God; and short, frequent prayer from the heart is better than attempting long and laborious prayers from a book. In prayer it is God's Holy Spirit at work in us who leads us.

5. **Keep one eye on others:** When we are locked away from others we often become lonely. And loneliness can lead to self-pity. Giving even a cup of cold water to others reminds us that we have something to give and so have something to be grateful to God for. Once there was a grieving woman who visited a holy man in China and asked him to help her overcome her sorrow. He told her she must obtain a mustard seed from a home that had never known sadness and it would banish her sorrow. The woman couldn't find such a home. Instead, wherever she visited, she was told of the tragic things that had happened there. On hearing each tale she asked herself, "Who is better able to help these people than I, who have known so much sorrow?" She became so involved at easing the grief and comforting others that she forgot about her search for the mustard seed which, in fact, had driven the sorrow from her life.

11. The Nurturing Spirit
The sacrament of the Eucharist

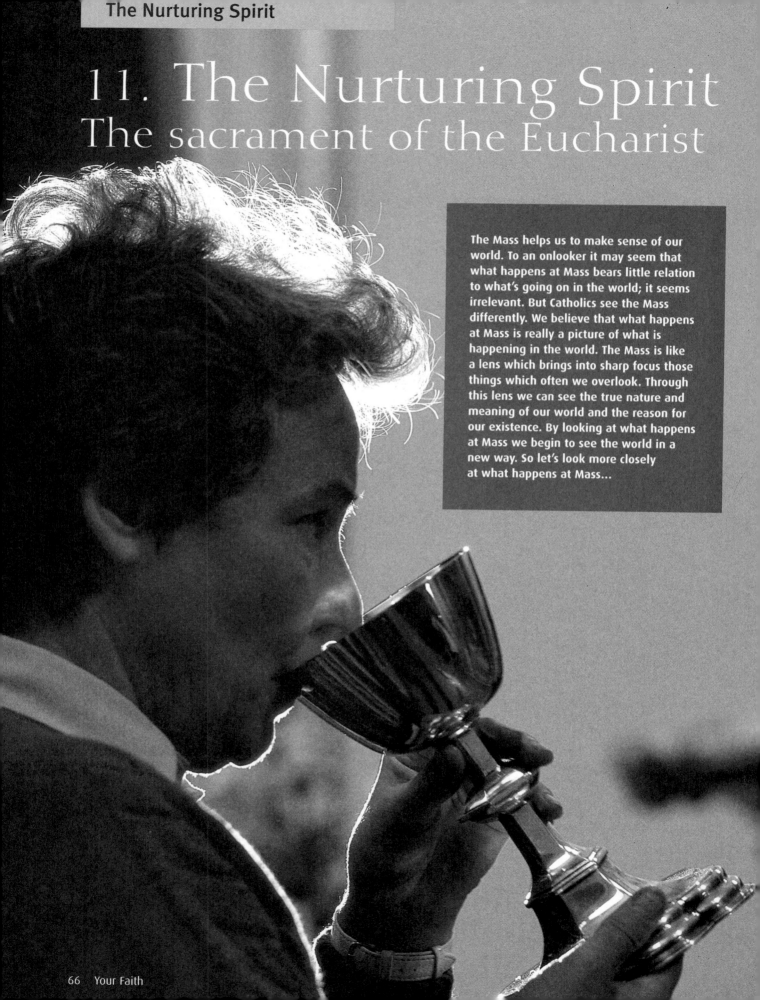

The Mass helps us to make sense of our world. To an onlooker it may seem that what happens at Mass bears little relation to what's going on in the world; it seems irrelevant. But Catholics see the Mass differently. We believe that what happens at Mass is really a picture of what is happening in the world. The Mass is like a lens which brings into sharp focus those things which often we overlook. Through this lens we can see the true nature and meaning of our world and the reason for our existence. By looking at what happens at Mass we begin to see the world in a new way. So let's look more closely at what happens at Mass...

Coming together

The first thing we see is people coming together. They come from different homes and situations: some happy, some sad, some fulfilled, some lonely. But there is a unity. Catholics are united in that we believe that coming together for the Sunday Eucharist, or Mass, is important. For we believe that, despite all the problems, God's power is at work in the world and that God's strength can overcome human weakness. This is true for people of every race, color, and creed. **Our coming together as Christ's followers brings this belief in God's power within each one of us into focus.**

Listening

The second thing we see at Mass is that very soon everyone sits down to listen to the Scriptures being read. There are a lot of ways in which we believe that God has spoken and continues to speak to people. Human experience and our own conscience, for example, are ways in which God touches everyone. Yet for Christians there is something more: there is Jesus Christ and all that he has taught us about God and his love for his people. That's why, at the final reading, which is from the Gospels, we stand to listen to the words Jesus himself spoke. **When we listen to God's word in the Scriptures it brings God's voice in the world into focus.**

Thanksgiving

The third thing we see as central to the Mass is what Catholics call the Eucharistic Prayer. The word "eucharist" comes from the Greek word meaning "thanksgiving." Everyone gathers around the altar with the priest to re-enact what Christ did with his disciples at the Last Supper. We listen afresh to Christ's words thanking and praising God saying, *"Take this, all of you, and eat it. This is my body which will be given up for you."* Then, *"Take this, all of you, and drink from it: this is the cup of my blood, the blood of the new and everlasting covenant. It will be shed for you and for all so that sins may be forgiven. Do this in memory of me."* We believe what Christ said. We believe that when we remember and act on his words, Jesus is present. This is the most precious moment of life. The bread and wine which has been brought forward to represent our life and work are now changed into the Body and Blood of Jesus Christ. He is present, as he said he would be, and is our reminder of

God's unending promise. But this precious moment doesn't mean that what's happening in the rest of the world is irrelevant. The opposite is true. This moment reminds us of the importance of every single person in God's eyes. **Our celebration of Christ's presence among us brings into focus just how precious is the whole of God's world.**

Communion

Finally, at the heart of the Mass is Holy Communion. This is a personal moment. When we share in this sacred meal we do indeed share in the life of Christ. We are experiencing the result of God's great desire to come to us and be one with us. To make the bread and wine for our communion, grapes and grain are crushed. Jesus Christ was also crushed for our communion. He was crushed and crucified on the cross, so that the power of God's love for all could be shown. In all our lives there is suffering, but our suffering is not meaningless. For when suffering is faced with love, that which is crushed and broken is transformd by such love into new life. **Our celebration of communion brings into focus the cost of all true loving and shows us where such love will lead us— into the hands of God the Creator of love.**

What does the Eucharist tell us?

When we think about the reality of what our celebration at Mass tells us, it becomes clear that in the Eucharist we find all that we need in life. We find unity with others, guidance from our heavenly Father, food for the journey, and confirmation of the promise which was made to us by Jesus Christ. The Lord has not the slightest intention of leaving us to our own devices and our narrow outlook on life. Having created each of us to be special and unique he doesn't leave it there any more than we would leave a newborn baby to fend for itself. No, our heavenly Father intends to nurture and pamper us every moment of our lives until the day we are completely one with him in love, unity, and peace.

God gives us his Body and Blood as a sign of his continued presence to nurture and continually form us in his likeness. We are called to bring Christ to our home, our workplace, our world. And we are called to do this, not by hollow words and empty gestures, but as Christ comes to us—in a simple, everyday way; a gentle way with ordinary, everyday gifts and actions which transform and nurture in a profound and authentic way.

Early days

From the earliest days the Christian community has come together to celebrate the Eucharist or, as it is often referred to, the Mass. The Acts of the Apostles, written around AD 70 tells how the early Christians met regularly for "the breaking of bread" (Acts 2:42). And in one of the most valuable documents we possess, Justin the Martyr gives us this unique picture of the celebration of Mass in AD 150:

"On the day which is called Sunday, all, whether they live in the town or the country, gather in the same place. Then the memoirs of the Apostles or the Writings of the Prophets are read for as long as time allows.

"When the reader has finished, the president speaks, exhorting us to live by these noble teachings.

"Then we rise together and pray. Then as we said earlier, when the prayer is finished, bread, wine, and water are brought. The president then prays and gives thanks as well as he can. And all the people reply with the acclamation, 'Amen.'

"Then the eucharistic gifts are distributed and shared out to everyone, and the deacons are sent to take them to those who are absent."

The Mass is a mystery which touches the life of the whole world. It is like an irresistible magnet which in the huge sprawling cities and the remotest villages stirs people out of their homes and groups them together around the Lord. The language can be different, the external shape and form can change, but the essence of the mystery remains always intact. Nothing has changed since Justin's day.

What is the Eucharist?

Christ's own preaching of the Eucharist met with small success. In the synagogue at Capernaum his claim that he would give his flesh for the life of the world was greeted very unsympathetically. Many of his followers walked away. And, at the Last Supper, with his closest disciples, when he took bread and wine, saying, "This is my body...this is my blood poured out for you," one of those with Jesus had the mind to betray him.

To the ancient world the Eucharist seemed "intolerable language" (John 6:60). It appears no more reasonable to the modern world. And so it has been throughout the Church's history. Jesus' claim seems to defy reason. "How can this man give us his flesh to eat?" How can it make sense to suggest that "Christ becomes present in this sacrament precisely by a change of the bread's whole substance into his body and the wine's whole substance into his blood"? (Saint Thomas Aquinas).

We must be clear about two things. First, in the Eucharist we are going beyond appearances. In the Eucharist Christ is as truly present as he was nearly two thousand years ago in Capernaum. And, even then, people judged only by external appearances. "This is the son of Joseph. We know his father and his mother," they said, "how can he claim to have come down from heaven?...What sign will you give to show us that we should believe in you?" Appearances were deceiving. Appearances are deceiving.

Second, Christ's presence among men and women was not in itself sufficient to save those who met him. To be saved, they had to approach him in faith. We have to communicate with him. He is present as our food, the eating of which gives us a share in his saving sacrifice and resurrection.

Yet Christ's presence among us, and especially his unique presence in the Eucharist, is the foundation of our faith. It is the mystery of faith. How does the Church describe the vital change which takes place in the bread and wine at the words of consecration at Mass?

Many Catholics are familiar with the word "transubstantiation," which has been used by the Church since the twelfth century to describe this change. The substance of the bread changes; but the accidents do not.

Accidents are those qualities which are perceived by the senses—taste, touch, sight, and so on. The substance is what is grasped by the mind. Only an intelligent human being can say "what" a thing is.

Usually, when the senses perceive the qualities of whiteness, softness, and so on, the mind, left to itself, says, "that is bread." But Jesus Christ has not left the mind to itself. He tells us that by the power of his word the bread and wine are changed into his Body and Blood.

Eucharist means thanksgiving

The eating of the bread and wine, which are changed into the Body and Blood of Jesus Christ to be the food of eternal life, is the sign of our union with Christ. In the synagogue in Capernaum Jesus said, "Anyone who does eat my flesh and drink my blood has eternal life and I shall raise him up on the last day" (John 6:54).

Jesus instituted the Eucharist within the Jewish passover meal on the night before he died. Jesus said, "I have longed to eat this passover with you before I suffer; for I shall not eat it again until it is fulfilled in the kingdom of God" (Luke 22:15-16).

Then Jesus took some bread, and when he had given thanks, broke it and gave it to them, saying,

"'This is my body which shall be given for you; do this as a memorial of me.' He did the same with the cup after supper, and said 'This cup is the new covenant in my blood which will be poured out for you.'"

In the Eucharist, then, we are united with Christ through the power of the Spirit and so united with the risen Christ's worship of his Father. "Nourished by his body and blood and filled with his Holy Spirit, we become one body, one Spirit in Christ" and so are able to offer glory and honor to the Almighty Father.

The Mass perpetuates Christ's sacrifice on the cross

The Mass is the same sacrifice as that of Calvary. This is the central mystery of our faith. But what does it mean? The casual observer sees no similarity whatever between the callousness of Calvary and the calmness of today's celebration. We will explain this sameness in three stages:

What happened at Calvary.
On the Cross, Jesus chose to offer himself to the Father, in the supreme sacrifice of the giving of his blood. At that moment Jesus breathed his last with the words, "Father, into your hands I commit my spirit."

But then, into Jesus' lifeless body the Father poured his life-giving Spirit. The Son, who offered his life into the hands of the Father, now sits at the right hand of his Father, raised up as Lord.

On the night before he died Jesus had instituted the Eucharist to be a sign of his true and continuing presence. To understand the full significance of his presence, we look at the full meaning of the sign.

What happens at Mass.
And what do we see? We see the sign of Christ's body and blood on our altar offered to the Father by the priest. In the name of Christ he consecrates the bread and wine,

changing them into Jesus' Body "given up for you" and Blood "shed for you."

On our altar at Mass, then, Christ is present in the moment of offering himself to his Father. Jesus Christ, filled with the life-giving Spirit of his Father, is given for us. What happens in a bloody manner on Calvary takes place in a sign, but just as truly, at Mass.

What is the difference between Christ's offering on Calvary and at Mass?
On Calvary, Jesus was offering directly in his own Person. But at Mass Jesus offers through the person of his priest and also in union with his followers, his Church.

On Calvary, suspended between heaven and earth, Jesus was alone, isolated from the men and women who had rejected him. But, at Mass, we are united with Christ's offering. We are part of his Body, the Church.

At Mass, in other words, Christ's offering becomes our offering; for in baptism we became members of Christ's Body. We are not spectators at the sacrifice of the Mass like the bored soldiers playing dice at Calvary, nor even like Mary and John looking up into the face of the dying Jesus. We are members of Christ's Body. We offer the sacrifice through him, with him, and in him.

I will not leave you orphans

Jesus had the nicest way of putting things. While preparing his first followers for his departure from this world, he told them, "I will not leave you orphans."

These words of Christ were particularly well chosen because when we think of orphans we see, in our mind's eye, forlorn and faltering children. And when we think of the apostles we see that at times they behaved not like little children but like big children. They argued among themselves as to who was the greatest—as to who was the "king of the castle." They made rash promises which they couldn't keep. They got frightened and ran away. Towards the end of his public life they caused an exasperated Jesus to exclaim, "Have I been with you all this time and you still don't understand?"

Of course, while he was with them, the apostles didn't understand. Indeed, they couldn't understand. For while Jesus was with them they could only remain helpless onlookers. Only when Jesus was gone could they begin, literally, to take his place.

Jesus had not only the nicest way of putting things, but also the nicest way of doing things. He promised that through his Spirit he would remain with the apostles and with us. But he would remain in a way that we could easily understand. He would remain through signs or sacraments.

Jesus Christ remains with us through the sign of what came to be known as the "laying on of hands." Present-day bishops, priests, and deacons, in their differing degrees, are ordained or impressed with the priestly character of Christ, by the imposition of hands.

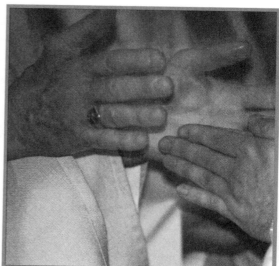

Deacons

Soon after Jesus' ascension a hierarchy of orders began to develop. We read in Acts how "seven men of good reputation" were elected for the daily distribution of alms in order that the apostles could be freed for "prayer and the service of the word." Their number included Stephen, the first Christian martyr who was stoned to death. The services performed by these men grew into the duties of the deacon.

In the early Church, deacons quickly became important as assistants to the bishops. But over the centuries their tasks were divided up and given to others. Today, their early caring role for the poor and the care of the finances of the community are usually delegated to lay people in the parish.

Yet the office of deacon didn't die out altogether. It was always a step, the last, before the priesthood, and Saint Francis of Assisi, for example, remained a deacon all his life. Today, with the reintroduction of the permanent diaconate, they are again becoming important in the life of the Church.

Deacons are chosen from a parish for work with the local priests or bishops. Most countries now have permanent deacons; some of these have other secular jobs, others make it a full-time vocation. In parishes where there are several Mass centers the deacon may organize one or other center. He can baptize, visit the people, witness marriages, bring communion to the sick, instruct the people, lead them in prayer, and generally be the leader and animator of the area where he lives.

12. The Trusting Spirit
The sacrament of Holy Orders

What is a priest?

The sacrament of holy orders confers the character of Jesus Christ in a special way. The ministerial priesthood is essentially different from the priesthood enjoyed by all those who are baptized, for the priest is empowered to "consecrate, offer, and administer the Body of Christ" for the good of the Church and of the world. The office of the priesthood is a sacrament in which, irrespective of human failing, Christ is made present. The stole (a long "scarf" worn over both shoulders) is a distinctive symbol of the priest's sharing in Christ's priesthood.

The priesthood is for the service of the Church. The priest is to gather and mold his community so that everyone may live and work in the communion of love which is the Church. In this the priest follows Jesus Christ who "came among us as one who serves." The celibacy of priests is a sign which enables them more freely to devote themselves to the service of God and men and women.

The priest is ordained, then, to act in the person of Jesus Christ. The fullness of the ministerial priesthood belongs to the bishop, who is assisted by priests and deacons. The ring worn by a bishop is a sign that he is wedded to his diocese.

The priest acts in the person of Jesus Christ in three principal ways:

- He teaches: The priests' first duty is the proclamation of the Gospel of God to all. In this way they fulfill the Lord's command, "Go out to the whole world; proclaim the Good News to all creation." Thus they establish and build up the People of God.

- He makes holy: Having sown the seed of faith through preaching, priests unite their people to God by the administration of the sacraments, especially the celebration of the Eucharist. Through the reception of the Eucharist the community of believers is joined to the Body of Christ.

- He governs: Having gathered together God's family into the one Body of Christ through the celebration of the sacraments, priests share in the office of Christ, the Leader and the Shepherd. Imitating him, priests lead those in their care to a deeper understanding of their own vocation and so build up a genuine Christian community.

Peter – leader of the apostles

Every group needs a leader, and so Jesus appointed Peter to a special position at the head of his people:

"So now I say to you: You are Peter and on this rock I will build my Church. And the gates of the underworld can never hold out against it. I will give you the keys of the kingdom of heaven; whatever you bind on earth shall be considered bound in heaven; whatever you loose on earth shall be considered loosed in heaven" (Matthew 16:18-19).

The apostles and early Christians certainly recognized Peter as the head of the Church. Not only does his name always appear at the head of any list of the apostles but he is expressly referred to as the leader in the early literature of the Church. It was Peter who presided over the election of Matthias, the replacement for the fallen Judas. He was the first to preach the Gospel openly and the first to take the controversial step of receiving a pagan convert into the new People of God. When Paul was starting his missionary activity, he first went to visit and confer with Peter in Jerusalem (Galatians 1:18).

The command to serve

There is no doubt at all that Peter and his fellow apostles were appointed to special positions of authority within the new People of God. We should be very careful to notice, however, just what Christ had to say about the way they should use this authority.

"You know that among the pagans the rulers lord it over them, and their great men make their authority felt. This is not to happen among you. No, anyone who wants to be great among you must be your servant, and anyone who wants to be first among you must be your slave, just as the Son of Man came not to be served but to serve, and to give his life as a ransom for many" (Matthew 20:25-28).

A few hours before he was crucified, Jesus took a towel and washed the feet of his disciples. There could be no mistaking his intention. The true follower of Christ, no matter what his position among the people, must always be the servant of others. And as the apostles set about organizing the Church, it was a command they were to keep very much in mind.

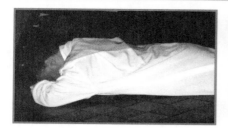

What happens at ordination?

- Those to be ordained gather together with their families, friends, and the Christian community to celebrate this sign of God's life in the world. Words of welcome are exchanged and an opening prayer said.
- Everyone present listens to the word of God read from the Scriptures.
- The candidates are called forward and are presented to the bishop.

- The bishop then elects or chooses the candidates for the priesthood and this choice is consented to by the Christian community who are present.
- Following a homily, the bishop asks the candidates four key questions to which they give an affirmative response:
  - Will they care for the Lord's flock?
  - Will they celebrate the mysteries of Christ faithfully?
  - Will they preach the Gospel?
  - Will they consecrate their lives to God for the salvation of his people?

- Each of the candidates now makes a promise of obedience to the bishop. Prayers are offered for the candidates.
- In silence the bishop lays his hands on the head of each candidate. This is followed by the solemn prayer of consecration.
- The bishop gives the kiss of peace to each of the new priests.
- The newly ordained priests are each invested with a stole and chasuble and their palms are anointed with Oil of Chrism.
- The liturgy of the Eucharist follows.

Ministries

The word "ministries" comes from the Latin word meaning "to render service." It is used in the Church not simply to describe the ordained ministry of the priesthood, but also to describe the different ways in which Catholics exercise functions within the Church. These reflect a deepening vision in the Church of the service given by all in the name of the Church.

A ministry has the ultimate aim of preaching and building up of the kingdom of God as revealed by Jesus Christ. Each baptized person is called to do this. Different tasks, some officially recognized and others unheralded, are undertaken by individuals to build up the community of believers. They are gifts, Saint Paul tells us, "to build up the body of Christ until we become one in faith and in the knowledge of God's Son."

How many ministries are there?

In a very real sense there is only one ministry—the ministry of Jesus Christ. It is Jesus Christ who reaches out to serve men and women through the members of his Body, the Church. To help our understanding of this, however, we speak of three different types of ministry:

- Ministries undertaken by those who are baptized. This refers to any activity which is undertaken without a formal commission from the Church. These ministries would include the work of nurses, teachers, and social workers. It is important to recognize that this type of ministry is not limited to the caring professions. It includes the service of all who work in their local parish and do everyday work in a spirit of Christian dedication.
- The instituted ministries. These are the ministries officially recognized as forms of service within the Church such as lectors, acolytes, catechists, ministers of the Eucharist.
- The ordained ministries are those of the diaconate, priesthood, and episcopate and are only exercised by those who have received the sacrament of Holy Orders.

The apostles: the foundations of the Church

We have seen that the origins of our faith are rooted in the Jewish people of the Old Testament. Jesus made it perfectly clear in his preaching that he had come not to destroy the hopes and desires of the Jewish people but to fulfill them. Tragically, only a few were convinced that the new People of God had come into existence with the community established by Jesus Christ.

Jesus chooses his apostles

For three years, Jesus traveled around preaching the good news of the kingdom of God, and began to gather around him a small group of followers whom he instructed very carefully. These men and women formed the nucleus of the new People of God.

It was from among this nucleus that Jesus chose twelve disciples to be the leaders of his Church. These men were to be the foundation members of his new people. They were to be sent out on his business and so he called them apostles: in Greek that is exactly what the word means, "those who are sent." After spending a whole night in prayer, Jesus named his apostles: Simon whom he called Peter, and his brother Andrew, James, John, Philip, Bartholomew, Matthew, Thomas, James son of Alphaeus, Simon called the Zealot, Simon son of James, and Judas Iscariot who became a traitor (Luke 6:14-16).

The choice of the twelve was full of meaning. In the Old Testament the chosen people are often referred to as the twelve tribes of Israel. Jesus was obviously underlining the real link between the new Israel and the old and stressing at the same time the continuity of God's plan.

The organization of the Church

The key to a true understanding of the organization of the Catholic Church is the command of Christ to serve. Saint Paul mentions in his letters various offices such as elders, presbyters, bishops, priests, and deacons. These men and women were given positions of authority in the new People of God. They were there to serve the people and not to lord it over them. In fact, the usual word used in the New Testament to refer to their authority is "diakonia," a word which means "service."

The organization of the Catholic Church is still based on the command of Christ to serve. It is an ideal which has been obscured many times by human greed and failure. Nevertheless, if we look at the Church today and in history, we can see a sincere effort on the part of many to put this command into practice.

Every member of the new People of God is called to a life of service. We must serve God by serving one another. But if our service is to be truly Christlike we need leaders to guide and organize our efforts. They, like the apostles before them, are our servants.

The pope

The pope, the Bishop of Rome, is often referred to as the "servant of the servants of God." He is the successor of Saint Peter and the visible leader of the Church on earth. He is the leader of many millions of Catholics but he leads only to serve them in imitation of Christ himself.

The college of bishops

Peter was the acknowledged leader of the group of apostles chosen by Christ. Just as the pope is the successor of Peter so are the bishops the direct successors of the apostles. They, like the apostles, have been chosen by Christ, and their authority comes from him. But their authority binds them to a life of service. As a group they must work for the whole Church and the conversion of the world. This they try to do in imitation of the apostles who worked closely together to take the message of Christ to the four corners of the earth.

"Each of them...is to be solicitous for the whole Church...to instruct the faithful in love for the whole mystical body of Christ, especially for its poor and sorrowing members and for those who are suffering persecution...and to supply to the missions both workers and also spiritual and material aid, and...to gladly extend their fraternal aid to other churches, especially to neighboring and more needy dioceses" (Vatican II).

The bishops

A bishop is the leader of a certain section of the People of God called a diocese. A diocese is the local Church and the members of this Church are served by the bishop in a special way.

"Bishops should dedicate themselves to their apostolic office as witnesses of Christ before all men. Their ultimate goal as bishops is that all may walk 'in goodness and justice and truth.'... In exercising his office as father and pastor a bishop should stand in the midst of his people as one who serves. Let him be a good shepherd who knows his sheep and whose sheep know him. Let him be a true father who excels in the spirit of love and solicitude for all and to whose divinely conferred authority all gratefully submit themselves" (Vatican II).

Priests and deacons

The bishop cannot possibly serve all the people of his diocese single-handed. The apostles, by laying on of hands, shared some of their powers and duties with priests and deacons. The bishops continue to ordain men and so share the burdens of their office.

The priest is the leader of a group of people within the diocese. He represents Christ in a special way and imitates him by giving the sacraments, preaching, and teaching.

A deacon serves the people by a life dedicated to charity and administration. He is ordained by the bishop and has power to baptize, to preach, and to conduct marriages and funerals.

The laity

Every member of the new People of God is called to serve. We have seen how the Holy Spirit lives in each of us, inspiring some to be leaders and teachers, while others have gifts for taking care of the sick and the poor. There are those who have the patience to do the smallest tasks well and still others with the perseverance and courage to tackle immense problems.

In short, there are many gifts given to us by the Holy Spirit. The important thing is that we use them in the service of God and our neighbor. This is the command Christ left to every member of his Church. For as members of his Church we have the responsibility of making Christ visibly present to those among whom we live and work. For the visible Church is not just the pope and the bishops and a world-wide organization. It is us. And if we don't make Christ present to the people we come into contact with, who else will?

The truth is that the followers of Jesus in every age are united to him in such a way that they form one body with him. With Jesus they are the Church. With them and through them Jesus continues the redeeming work he came to do on earth. Just as Jesus made God visibly present to the men and women of his time so now the Church which he founded, and of which he is the head, makes Jesus present to the men and women of today.

Please Join Us For A Celebration of Marriage

What happens at a wedding?

- The couple, their families, friends, and the Christian community gather together to celebrate this sign of God's life in the world. Words of welcome are exchanged and opening prayers are offered for the couple and their future happiness.
- Everyone present listens to the word of God read from the Scriptures.
- The couple are asked three questions which cover the key elements of Christian marriage:

Total giving
"Have you come here freely and without reservation to give yourselves to each other in marriage?"

Total faithfulness
"Will you love and honor each other as man and wife for the rest of your lives?"

Creative love
"Will you accept children lovingly from God and bring them up according to the law of Christ and his Church?"

An affirmative response is given to each question by each person.

- The couple then declare their consent to the marriage before God and his people. They publicly unite themselves for life in this Christian marriage.
- Wedding rings are exchanged as a sign of the vows that have been taken and as a sign that their commitment is unending.
- Prayers are offered by everyone present for the couple, for their families, for all married people, and for the whole world.
- A celebration of the Eucharist may follow.

13. The Sharing Spirit
The sacrament of marriage

The touch of love

There is an old eastern proverb which says, "One look is worth a dozen words and one touch is worth a dozen looks." It's true. Even the lightest touch speaks volumes. It can lift us into another world—the world of love.

A desire to marry is a sign that each partner has been "touched" by another in an extra special way. They have opened their hearts to each other and finally found the courage in their love to want to offer and to receive total commitment for life. There is a risk here for they are offering their whole life to another human being in complete trust. But love, the kind of authentic love which reflects the love of God, does just that; it is willing to give everything, even life itself, for the beloved.

Such a magnificent reflection of God's love is almost too much for us to understand. People often say that they don't understand what a couple see in each other. But love makes it possible for us to see what no one else sees except God, that the one who is loved is uniquely precious, irreplaceable, and infinitely lovable. It is natural that those who experience such love want to tell the world and want their love to continue forever.

That is what is at the heart of Christian marriage; that is what is announced to the world on the wedding day. And in that announcement each partner touches the other in a special way; at the heart of the ceremony, the couple take each other's hand and exchange rings as a sign that their love is for life. From that moment on, as they touch each other in their love-making, they will re-create their own lives and create a new family as partners with God in the world.

The wedding day completes one period of a relationship and begins another. The love which has been acknowledged and publicly announced, now begins to grow and nurture each partner. This takes place in a variety of ways because every marriage is unique. If we look at our hands, the hands which exchange one of the first signs of "touch," we can see how each finger bears its own print—unrepeated on anyone else, ever, at any time.

It's been said that, "like fingerprints, all marriages are different." Each marriage is special, no marriage on earth is quite like another. Regardless of the kind of family a couple come from, their parents' marriage, or the kind of marriage they are "expected" to have, the partners of each marriage have the right and the call from God to create a marriage that is right for them—based on that unconditional love announced at their wedding.

Sex and love

When we talk about "making love" we usually mean sexual intercourse between two people. But if we stop to think about it, "making love" is much more than that. Sexual intercourse can just be a selfish ego trip or simply a desire to follow the crowd. But sexual intercourse is transformed when, in marriage, it becomes a sign of the special love of the couple. This is a love which shows itself in lifelong commitment to one another, in unselfishness, and which, after tension or disagreement, can share genuine forgiveness. This love, expressed in sexual intercourse, is creative in two ways:

- **Each partner re-creates the other:** Perhaps for the first time they feel really free and have the trust to share themselves honestly and openly. Each may bring to the marriage scars from earlier relationships or from childhood. Love in marriage helps to heal these hurts. It offers the chance to start again. In the safety of each other's arms, each discovers the liberation of true security, new depths, new values. Such experiences transform each partner and help their love to last.

- **New life is created:** A special and unique sign of love-making is the creation of a completely new human being. The future of that child will depend very much on the quality of the love in the couple's life together.

God and love

It's so much easier to believe in someone's love for us when we feel their arms about us. The touch of a partner reassures us of their love. It should also reassure us of God's love since Christians believe that God reaches out and touches us through the love of others. Jesus Christ is at the heart of all love.

Falling in love is a very human experience. But when we decide to consecrate that love in Christian marriage our human love becomes a sign in the world of God's love. Our experience tells us that there is something "extra" here—something beyond human explanation. When we pledge ourselves to unconditional love for life we show what Christ's own self-sacrificing love is like. Ours, like his, is a love without limits. We are in true partnership with God.

It's not surprising, then, that God does offer us his own supreme love to strengthen and sustain us and to make perfect love possible. That is what is at the heart of Christian marriage. This mystery and miracle of love, the sacrament of marriage, is indeed a partnership with God. God is involved, intimately, in the relationship.

Marriage to someone who isn't a Catholic

Many Catholics marry someone who belongs to a different church or who has no religious beliefs. It's important that such couples take time to understand each other's point of view on all religious and domestic matters. Each partner is called to respect the other's point of view and must allow them the freedom to practice their faith.

It's also important that the partner who isn't a Catholic knows and understands the obligations the Catholic has to keep his or her own faith and to bring up any child they might have in that faith. It's important, too, that the Catholic understands and respects the religious views of their partner with sincere reverence.

The obligations of the Catholic are expressed in the promise made before the wedding,

"I declare that I am ready to uphold my Catholic faith and to avoid all dangers of falling away from it. Moreover, I sincerely undertake that I will do all that I can within the unity of our partnership to have all the children of our marriage baptized and brought up in the Catholic Church."

Marriage vs. Living together

Many people think that living together or a "trial marriage" is the best form of marriage preparation. It's only by living with someone, they say, that you can really get to know them properly.

Certainly couples who live and sleep together get to know a lot about each other. But it is very different from marriage in one big way. A trial marriage is temporary. If things go wrong the couple will split up. Christian marriage is permanent. When things go wrong the couple will stick together and work things out.

For Christians, married love is like Christ's love; it is faithful and unselfish and permanent. An arrangement in which a couple agree to "live together" and to separate if things go wrong, inevitably devalues the love they profess because it brings to their relationship some self-interest and infidelity.

Living together makes a statement which says, "I will be with you as long as it is right for me....I will stay with you while I am happy with you....I do not love you enough to commit my life to you but you'll do for now...." Such a value system devalues self-esteem, reduces each partner to a conditional love that must come up to scratch or be rejected. That way of dealing with people and with human relationships is very damaging to individuals and to a couple. Such an arrangement appears to lend freedom to a relationship, but it also breeds insecurity and lack of confidence. What happens in sickness and unemployment, in the care of children or in old age? These are the reasons for Christ's clear teaching that life together in a sexual union belongs only in marriage.

Marriage
Sacrament with a difference

In one respect, at least, the sacrament of marriage is different from the other six sacraments. Unlike the others, marriage is recognized as an essential part of secular society. Get rid of all religion, in other words, and marriage still makes sense.

This cannot be said of the other six sacraments. Baptism, the Eucharist, reconciliation, and so on, are religious rites. They can only be celebrated as signs of our faith in God.

It is essential to recognize this in order to understand the sacrament of marriage and the laws which surround it. For it helps to explain the changes that have taken place in the marriage laws over the centuries. And, of more practical importance, it helps us to understand the changes that are taking place in the Church's marriage legislation today. To a great extent our understanding of marriage and the church laws that govern its celebration are colored by changes in society.

For the first thousand years of the Church's history no special church ceremony was considered necessary for the majority of Christians. In the first centuries this fact, of course, is hardly surprising. Many were married as pagans and baptized as Christians afterwards. And it never occurred to the remainder who married after baptism to have a separate church ceremony distinct from the normal "civil" marriage celebrated in the family or immediate social circle. Yet marriage between Christians was recognized as a holy union of men and women in Christ, "celebrated by God himself in heaven."

Sometimes church ceremonies accompanied the "civil" ceremony. But, generally, marriage followed the form of local custom, which varied from region to region. And in practice the Church accepted the power of the state to pass most of the necessary marriage laws, including those affecting Christians.

From the eleventh century we detect a distinct change in the Church's policy. After long centuries of confusion following the crumbling of the Roman Empire people needed order and stability. And the Church fulfilled that need. She helped to reconstruct society by taking over marriage in its civil forms and so acquired virtually exclusive legal powers in matrimonial affairs.

This was a lengthy process. It was not until 1560 that the Church finally insisted on marriage being solemnized in the presence of a priest and two witnesses, and the results were mixed.

It was a civilizing process in that, for example, the Church slowly but successfully fought the practice by which the father literally "gave away" his daughter in marriage as he would dispose of any property. On the other hand, the process meant that the Church and the civil authorities tended to go their separate ways, with unfortunate consequences for both.

We have already seen that marriage is different from the other sacraments; marriage is an essential part of secular society. One fact emphasizes this. Alone in the Church's liturgy and from the earliest times all the marriage ceremonial of the Church has been celebrated in the local language of the people. It is the sacrament which, above all, must be understood.

Over the centuries society has colored our understanding of marriage but equally, and perhaps more importantly, over the centuries Christian marriage has changed society. And that is why the continuous interweaving of society and marriage, and the subtle change and adaptation which that stimulates, continues today. Christian marriage always has something "extra" to offer society and so the Church continues to be sensitive to the many new tensions and challenges in marriage that present themselves in every age.

The wedding ring

Rings have always been rich in symbolism. In biblical times they were made of ivory, crystal, or metal and were a sign of dignity and rank. Increasingly, they signified a pledge of loyalty and trust and, in Roman times, were used as a mark of betrothal.

Since the Middle Ages it has been traditional for the bridegroom to place the ring on the thumb of the bride, then on her second finger, and then on her third, naming each person in the Trinity. The ring was then placed on the fourth finger at the word, "Amen." This shows in action as well as in words that he enters marriage "in the name of the Father and of the Son and of the Holy Spirit."

Another reason in ancient times for placing the ring on the fourth finger is because it was believed that it contained a certain vein which proceeds to the heart. The ring is not a symbol of captivity; rather of unbroken unity and unending changelessness—the perfect round. It does not mean that "this person belongs to me" but "I belong to this person."

Rings at a wedding are blessed with these or similar words:

Lord, bless these rings which we bless in your name.
Grant that those who wear them may always have
a deep faith in each other.
May they do your will and always live together
in peace, goodwill, and love.
Through Christ our Lord. Amen.

To understand our humanity, what it is to be human, we need to look at Jesus Christ. Jesus was truly God; he was the Son who lived among us as a fully human person. He was exactly the same as us in all things. He ate like us, he laughed and cried like us, he loved like us, and his body was vulnerable and could suffer and be destroyed as ours can.

The only difference between Jesus' humanity and ours was that sin played no part in his life. He did not sin. And the reason he did not sin was because he was truly human. He was fully human exactly as God had intended every man and woman to be. He is a pattern for humanity. Jesus shows us what it is to be a true and complete human being.

14. The Healing Spirit
The sacrament of reconciliation

Sin enters our life when we are less than human. Every time we think, say, or do something which is not a reflection of Jesus' humanity, we are less than human; we sin. But sin doesn't stop there, because so much of what we do or fail to do affects other people. The chain reaction of damaging relationships, isolation, and breakdowns in communication all serve to cut us off from others and so distort and damage people. We even say in extreme cases, "He/she's like an animal!" What we're saying when we say that is in a sense true—that person is less than fully human—but then so are those who caused that distortion or damage, that isolation. It's easy to see that sin damages not only individuals but also whole communities.

Throughout his life Jesus worked and preached endlessly among all sorts of people to bring down the barriers which divided them. He emphasized over and over again that we are all God's children, we are his family, his chosen people.

Following his resurrection, Jesus' followers gathered together and became a community. They were united in that they were listening to the words of Jesus and experiencing his active love in the work of his Spirit in their lives. They knew what it was to be fully human but they were also still very weak and easily discouraged.

Even in the first accounts of the early Church we can read about tensions, disagreements, and rejection within this community of believers. Clearly, in spite of all that they had experienced, they remained fragile, and many of them carried within them the damage caused by sin (by being less than human) from past years.

No one becomes fully human overnight or even in a year or two. It takes time. And while we are growing towards full humanity we need to experience the healing, reconciling action of the Holy Spirit. The Church celebrates that action in the sacrament of reconciliation.

Through this sacrament we are renewed and recommitted to being open to the action of the Spirit in our lives in helping us to become more fully human and so be effective in reflecting Christ and his words of life and love to others. In this way we strengthen Christ's Body on earth, his community, which in turn can continue the healing, saving, loving work of Jesus Christ (see Luke 7:39-48).

Are we getting too casual about sin?
Concern is expressed in some quarters that people don't seem to go to confession anymore. There's a suggestion of laxity, a suggestion that Catholics are getting too casual about sin. At a recent discussion about general absolution someone remarked that if that became common practice nobody would go to individual confession at all—it would be an easy way of letting people off the hook. The unspoken suggestion here was that it was good for us to feel uncomfortable, to squirm, to suffer. It's interesting to note, when we hear this kind of comment, that when individual, private confession was first introduced in the Middle Ages by Irish missionary monks, it was at first condemned as a new form of permissive novelty.

Our healing God working in and through us
What is really behind so much of the debate and questioning about confession is that too many people find it either a burden or a waste of time. That's a pity because both those reservations and many of the ways in which we approach this sacrament have absolutely nothing to do with the reality of what is taking place.

When we take part in the celebration of any of the sacraments, we are making a statement. We are saying that we believe in God and in his all-embracing and redeeming love for us. We are publicly acknowledging this and we are saying to ourselves and to others that God is real in our lives, that the power and influence of the Holy Spirit is working within us, transforming us, strengthening us, enabling us to become more and more Christlike. That doesn't mean we are changing our personality; God has made each of us unique and special. Rather, he is perfecting, completing what has begun in our responses to his invitations as we move through life.

As one writer put it, the sacraments are not simply a "holy elevator" to the "heavenly floor." They are a genuine sign of what we are; people of faith and love, caught up in commitment to our heavenly Father.

Our healing God is realistic
In the sacrament of reconciliation God is being realistic, too, about what we are. We are weak. We are easily given to blindness, selfishness, and cruelty, to ourselves and others. We need help with these damaging traits; otherwise we will be overcome by them and be destroyed, lost in our own vanity, self-worship, and all-consuming blindness. We trail off along our own byways, leaving the Gospel and the love of God on the edge of our life. We begin to destroy ourselves, we begin to destroy others, we begin to destroy the kingdom of God which Jesus came to bring to all people.

Our healing God is always present

God's crazy love for us means that he cannot allow that to happen. He can't leave us to our own devices, our own clever little solutions. He reaches out endlessly to touch our coldness and our isolation into selfhood. In the sacrament of reconciliation he reassures us of his love, of his healing forgiveness—everything is safe, we are not lost, we are not rejected. God's great love for us overcomes even the worst sins we have committed, even our most pathetic failure. God has made everything better the moment we turned to him for help and forgiveness. In the sacrament of reconciliation, we are given the sign, the confirmation of what has already taken place.

If this sacrament is such a sign of love and welcome then why has it got such a poor image? Why is it something we make jokes about, avoid, or even hate? What's happening?

What do we say to our loving God?

The absolute and total secrecy surrounding this sacrament leads most of us to wonder what other people say in confession. And we wonder ourselves if we are saying the right things. The Church calls this sacrament "reconciliation" or "penance," but most Catholics still call it "confession" because confessing our sins seems the most important part of the sacrament. We can be nervous about confessing our sins for a variety of reasons.

1. We have neglected the sacrament for a long time and we don't know how to begin making a confession. In other words, we're rather like the lost son in the parable of the Prodigal Son, who hardly knew what to say to express his years of failure as he returned to his father.
2. We have committed a grave sin which we're ashamed of. In other words, we're rather like Peter with Jesus after his resurrection who is facing his own betrayal and Jesus' direct question, "Simon, son of John, do you love me more than these others do?"
3. We find ourselves confessing the same old sins as usual and so wonder if the Lord is as bored with our list of failures as we are. We're rather like the small boy who, told by his mother to say his night prayers, rather grumpily knelt down by the bed and said, "Dear God, same things as last night. Amen."

What do we say to our loving God?

All these "worries" have one thing in common. They are all centered on the confessing of our sins. They are concerned with what we have to say. And that's a very big mistake.

There are two people in every celebration of the sacrament—the penitent and Jesus Christ himself, who is present in his priest. The most important words are not what we say but the words of welcome and forgiveness which come from Jesus Christ. And so let's look again at

Situation 1

When we have neglected God for a long time the most important words are those of our Father in heaven who, even before we have offered our prepared speech, eagerly embraces us and announces that "we are going to have a feast, a celebration, because this child of mine was dead and has come back to life; was lost and is found" (Luke 15:24).

Situation 2

When we have been guilty of a serious or shameful sin the most important words are those of Jesus who, having given us the chance to say how much we love him, invites us to "Follow me." This is an invitation to follow him in his cross but to share, also, in his glory (John 21:19).

Situation 3

When we are guilty of the "same old sins" the most important words are, once again, those of Jesus who says, "If your brother does something wrong reprove him and, if he is sorry, forgive him. And if he wrongs you seven times a day and seven times comes back to you and says 'I am sorry' you must forgive him" (Luke 17:3-4).

These words of God can all be summarized in the one word, "Peace." This is Jesus' greatest gift to us offered on the day of his resurrection when he breathed into the apostles and his Church his Holy Spirit, saying, "Peace be with you....For those whose sins you shall forgive, they are forgiven" (John 20:21-23).

In our sorrow we are healed

When we celebrate the sacrament of reconciliation, then, we shouldn't concentrate too greatly on what we say to the priest. The Church reminds us that "the most important act of the penitent is contrition which is heartfelt sorrow along with the intention of sinning no more." In other words, "sorrow" in our heart is far more important than the way we express our sorrow.

And if our sorrow is less than perfect, it is within this sacrament that it is purified. Nothing brings home to us more forcefully the damage done to ourselves and others by sin than our reflection on Christ's own all-embracing, generous love in this sacrament.

What happens at the sacrament of reconciliation?

- The penitent and the priest meet to celebrate this sign of God's life in the world. Words of welcome are exchanged and an opening prayer is offered.

- The penitent listens to the word of God read from the Scriptures.

- The penitent acknowledges past failures and past refusals to live as a Christian. Personal sorrow is expressed.

- Words of encouragement are offered by the priest and a reminder of Christ's healing, welcoming love is given. A suggestion of an act of sorrow and reparation is made.

- An act of contrition is offered by the penitent in the form of a short prayer.

- The priest extends his hand and says the words of absolution:

    "God, the Father of mercies,
    through the death and resurrection of his Son
    has reconciled the world to himself
    and sent the Holy Spirit
    among us for the forgiveness of sins;
    through the ministry of the Church
    may God give you pardon and peace
    and I absolve you from your sins
    in the name of the Father,
    and of the Son, and of the Holy Spirit."

- A final prayer of praise and thanksgiving to God is offered.

    Note: In ceremonies of reconciliation involving a large group of people there are slight variations in the way that sins are acknowledged and past failures expressed.

15. The Saving Spirit
The sacrament of the sick

When we are sick, we feel alone, weak, and frightened. Things which seemed important don't matter much anymore. But as Christians we know that we are never alone. In fact we are never so close to Jesus as when we are weak or unwell.

During his life on earth, Jesus loved people into total health. He fought pain and suffering in himself and others. He lifted up those who were sick and raised them to new life.

Only when he could no longer avoid pain and death did Jesus accept it. And then, on the cross, Jesus transformed suffering. Through suffering he was raised to new life. And Jesus offers the same life to all who accept him in faith.

Throughout our lives Jesus loves us into total health, helping us to triumph over our sicknesses. For at the heart of being a Christian are the healing sacraments in which Jesus comes to us as a constant source of strength and restoration.

■ In baptism we join the family of God and celebrate God's love and care for us.

■ In reconciliation, we experience the healing power of Jesus Christ and the peace of mind which only he can give.

■ In the Eucharist we are strengthened and supported by the true presence of Jesus every time we turn to him.

The anointing of the sick is the ultimate healing sacrament, available whenever our health is seriously impaired by sickness, injury, or old age. God is always with us in our illness, loving us into health of mind, body, and soul. Through our faith we know that we will have life forever.

Throughout his life Jesus loved people so deeply and so completely that they were healed of whatever was destroying them, whether that was physical or mental illness, or emotional or spiritual suffering. That is what he continues to do when we receive the sacrament of the sick.

Our fears for the future begin to dissolve as we listen to the words of Jesus who promises to be with us forever.

Through this sacrament, sick people are strengthened and encouraged as they face any anxiety or fear they may have about frailty or death. Faith is renewed and the tendency in illness to despair and hopelessness is overcome by the loving signs of the Lord's presence at this special time in our lives.

Old age

The frailty of old age is recognized too. An old person may not be ill but the years do impose burdens upon the elderly which can be difficult to adjust to and which can make the older person feel isolated and at times very lonely. Again, this sacrament helps and strengthens the Christian in this stage of life so that they can continue to be part of the family of God as actively as possible, for older people have so much to offer younger Christians.

Children

A sick child has special difficulties to overcome. The normal activity and liveliness of youth are often limited to a considerable extent through illness. Being confined to bed or to the house for long periods can limit social contact with other children, and sick children can often worry about the stress their illness places upon parents and the rest of the family. The sacrament of the sick is for any sick children who are old enough to understand what it means and how it can help them as a sign of the real involvement of Jesus Christ in their life day by day.

A sign of life

Some people have the idea that this sacrament is rather like the sign of death or approaching death—it is only offered when all hope is lost. In fact the reverse is true; it is a sign of life, the eternal life promised by Jesus Christ, here and now as well as in the future. Christ came to show us how we can have life to the full in whatever situation we find ourselves. His Spirit, active and dynamic in our sickness and frailty as well as in our health and strength, is a real presence. The sacrament of the sick confirms this in a tangible way.

The final blessing of the sick person following reception of the sacrament of the sick is:

May God the Father bless you.
May God the Son heal you.
May God the Holy Spirit enlighten you.
May God protect you from harm and grant you salvation.
May he shine on your heart and lead you to eternal life.

God is with the sick person now, nothing is more certain than that. Throughout his life Jesus loved people so deeply and completely that they were healed of whatever was destroying them, whether that was physical or mental illness, or emotional or spiritual suffering. That is what he continues to do when we receive the sacrament of the sick.

In our growing closeness to Christ through faith celebrated in this sacrament we receive a new vision of life, a vision that sees everything in the light of God's eternal love. This love is lasting; no sickness is final and even death cannot withstand such love. When we are anointed with oil, a symbol of healing in Christ's time, we receive a sign of Christ's healing care for us now. It is only his strength that can lift us out of suffering to joy and peace.

> *"Any one of you who is ill should send for the elders of the church, and they must anoint the sick person with oil in the name of the Lord and pray over him. The prayer of faith will save the sick person and the Lord will raise him up again; and if he has committed any sins, he will be forgiven."*
>
> James 5:14-15

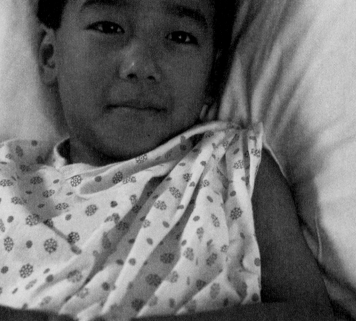

The Saving Spirit

What happens at the anointing of the sick?

This sacrament may be celebrated at the church either during a celebration of the Eucharist or at a service for those who are sick. More frequently, it is celebrated at home, during a house Mass or in a hospital or nursing home.

■ The family, friends, and Christian community gather together with the priest. Words of welcome are exchanged and all present are blessed with holy water.

■ In preparation for the sacrament, all who are present call to mind their personal failure to live as Christians. Prayers of sorrow and reconciliation are expressed.

■ Everyone listens to the word of God read from the Scriptures.

■ A series of short prayers and a litany are offered for all who are sick and for the person receiving the sacrament.

■ Following Christ's instructions, the priest lays his hands on the sick person in silence.

■ The sick person is then anointed on the forehead and the hands as the priest prays for him or her.

■ Everyone present prays the Lord's Prayer and Holy Communion may now be distributed. This is followed by a final prayer of blessing and healing.

The laying on of hands

After speech and facial expressions, the most powerful vehicle of human communication must surely be the hands. Dictators use sawing, sweeping gestures to the tumultuous roars of an hysterical crowd. The hands of a conductor chart rhythmic movements as the orchestra is guided at one moment into soft and peaceful melodies, at another into passionate *fortissimos*. When the police officer raises his or her hand the traffic comes to a halt. A wave says good-bye or welcome home. A caressing hand says, "You are beautiful." An embrace says, "I love you."

The liturgy of the Church is full of bodily gestures that are rich in meaning but may easily escape our notice. The laying on of hands in the sacrament of the sick is such a gesture. When, after the introduction, the priest places his hands on the sick person's head for a few moments, no words are spoken. There is complete silence. What does that mean? The gesture itself is borrowed from Jewish tradition and it has many meanings. It is a sign of blessing, as when Jacob blessed the sons of Joseph (Genesis 48:14). It is also a sign that the Spirit of God is coming to consecrate someone for a special task, for example, priests (Numbers 8:10).

Another meaning is that it is a symbol of union: when a sacrifice was to be offered, those making the offering would lay their hands on the victim as if to say, "I am one with you;

you are to take on my sentiments of thanksgiving or sorrow or adoration; and so, I will be united with you when you are offered in sacrifice" (Leviticus 1:4ff).

Some of these meanings are still preserved in the other sacraments like baptism, reconciliation, confirmation, and ordination. In the sacrament of the sick, the laying on of hands has a special meaning. First of all, it signifies blessing and healing. Jesus blessed the children in this way, he cured the woman afflicted with a painful stoop and restored sight to the blind man at Bethsaida. He promised that his disciples "will lay hands on the sick and they will be healed" (Mark 16:18). Straight away we see this practice in the early Church. After Saint Paul had become blinded, Ananias comes and lays his hands on him and his sight is restored (Acts 9:12).

So when the priest lays his hands on the sick person's head, he is following the instructions of Jesus and the practice of the apostles. He is praying, not with words but with a gesture, for healing. The healing, of course, will not be brought about just by a gesture or even by the priest. The gesture or action is what we see. What we don't see is the internal, hidden thing that is happening. The Spirit of God is released in the sick person who is disposed to receive the Spirit. The Spirit of God comes with healing and peace for the body, mind, and soul. For the Spirit, after all, was called "the Comforter" by Jesus.

Our final communion in this life, which we may receive when we are seriously ill or dying, is called the Viaticum, which means "the way." It is the way to eternal life, to our heavenly Father, in perfect peace.

Our first invitation to become a member of God's family was accepted at our baptism and confirmed by us at our confirmation. We have had the life of Christ within us strengthened continually through Holy Communion and many of us have received special help in living our vocations in marriage or holy orders. When we have turned away from God, grown weak, careless, and unloving, we have been continually welcomed back to our heavenly Father's family through the sacrament of reconciliation. In old age or sickness we have been healed from any spiritual ill and sometimes healed physically too, if this would be of benefit to us spiritually, by the sacrament of the sick.

16. Reborn in the Spirit
The death of a Christian

At the end of our life it is time to go home. God has kept his promise to us all of our life. He will always remain faithful...

There is a great consolation in our faith for anyone who has suffered the sadness and pain which accompanies the death of someone we love. For the faithful, life is changed, not ended, and the bond of union in the Body of Christ unites us still.

We can see that death to some extent is natural, since everything that lives on this earth dies if only to allow new life to spring up. That does not take away its pain. God did not make men and women to die. In fact, at first sight, the philosopher who said that death is absurd would seem to be right.

Life is of God
But then we read Saint Paul, and we learn that death came into this world because of sin. That explains it. The only real life is of God. And his creatures are privileged to share it. When any creature tries to make itself independent of God then it loses life. To be without God is to be dead. The wages of sin is death.

Death became the hallmark of human nature once people sinned. The Son of God became man so he took on the hallmark of human nature. He died because of sin. Now this is the miracle; he took our nature willingly, lovingly, and accepted death as its price. And his love was such that death could not triumph over it. Christ's death defeated death itself. That is what makes the cross of Christ the sign of victory over sin, because it was victorious over death. Christ took men and women back to his Father. This meant he showed his love for his Father by giving his life totally. His death, then, was the way through to the Father, a steppingstone to the Father. Death could no longer have the last word; it had lost its sting. Death had become the gateway to the life of the resurrection. That does not take away the pain of the cross, but it gives it purpose. Love is shown in pain, and the one who loves greatly suffers much.

The Christian is not better than Jesus Christ, nor has any other way to the Father been found but by the same way of the cross. For some it is a light burden, for others heavy, but it is for everyone. Everyone must die, but we do it by stages. It is Saint Paul who tells us that we have died already in baptism. It is clear what he means; we have died to sin. We must have, because we have begun to share in the new life of Christ risen from the dead.

That is what being a Christian means—sharing his life, literally. If we have risen, we must have died. Yes, we have died to sin, not finally, unfortunately, and that is the root of the problem. We can still sin, until the day we finally die. But every day, in trying to die a little more to sin, the Christian lives more deeply in Christ.

If we make a success of that, dying in the end won't be a problem. It will simply be the confirmation of our whole life's purpose. Death will not break our union with Christ but will establish it forever.

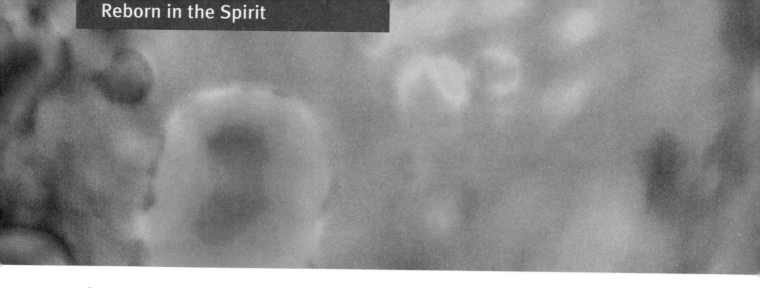

Judgment

"Judgment" sometimes conveys images of a balancing act on the heavenly scales of justice with the good actions of our lifetime on the one side and the bad ones on the other. Or we think of the judgment as a trial in which God sums up, while we listen in agonized suspense, and then passes a decision which could have us dragged away screaming for mercy or protesting our innocence. But judgment is not like that at all.

The truth is that we will be our own judge. And we save or condemn ourselves according to the way we judge Christ. Such is the power of Christ's words that our salvation or condemnation depends on our reaction to them. If we believe in Christ's words and accept them they will fill us with eternal life. But if we reject his words they will destroy us.

Go into a room on a summer evening when the sun is streaming through the window. The rays of the sun light up the room in a way that no artificial light can; everything seems transformed. But within those rays of light every little speck of dust and every little mark shows up with amazing clarity. The air about us is full of activity and hidden elements.

Only by drawing a curtain and keeping out the bright sunlight can we eliminate such an exposure by the light.

The words of Christ have the power of light. They show us what is in a man or woman, but some cannot accept it. They try to "draw a curtain" to shut out the light that is Christ. "You want to kill me," says Jesus, "because nothing I say has penetrated into you" (John 8:37).

It is a sad truth that so often we resent the goodness in other people. Their virtue shows up our own faults and failings and so we try to bring them down to size—our size. We behave, indeed, as Christ's accusers did. We judge. And by our judgment we are condemned with our own lips.

It would be wrong, therefore, to fear judgment as we fear the unknown. Judgment—and heaven or hell which follows—is known to us only too well. If our present life is one of hatred, of vengeance, walled up from the care of others, we are already experiencing something of the agony of hell. Our rejection of God and goodness, because we prefer selfishness and sin, can only lead to a continuation of the world we have built up for ourselves in eternity. Men and women are not cast into hell; they themselves create it.

Where does purgatory fit in?

There is a well-established tradition in the Church of praying for the dead but why is that considered necessary? Isn't the purpose of life on earth seen as a preparation for life after death and for becoming fit for heaven, for eternal life?

From experience we know that life often leaves a person incomplete, spiritually. Death can come when we are not quite ready to share in that full life with God in heaven. The Church has consistently held to the existence of purgatory as a state of purification for men and women prior to entering heaven.

The problem for many people is what is meant by "purification." In the preface for the Mass for the dead we are reminded that, in death, life is changed not ended. And at the heart of our faith there is the strong belief that through the mercy and justice of God, so clearly illustrated in the Gospels, all will end well.

Those in purgatory are removed from all distractions, illusions, and weaknesses of the human condition. Their whole being is turned towards God with an intense longing that only he can satisfy. So, the pain of "suffering souls" is one of longing to be finally united with God.

Although those in purgatory are described as "poor" or "suffering," the keynote of this teaching is in fact joy. For they are certain of the prize of heaven, there is no doubt about that. Through the prayers of all God's family they are encouraged and healed from all that hinders their complete unity with their heavenly Father.

The Church's teaching on purgatory confirms yet again the everlasting love, patience, and mercy of God in offering each of his beloved children every opportunity that they may need to be one with him in an eternal life of love and completeness.

On the other hand, if our present life is one of trying to receive Christ's words by accepting his brothers and sisters, even to the extent of "giving a cup of cold water in his name," we need have no fear of what follows judgment. Christ's words of welcome will show us up for what we are, "Come, you whom my Father has blessed, take for your heritage the kingdom prepared for you since the foundation of the world" (Matthew 25:34).

The communion of saints

A saint, from the Latin *sanctus* meaning "holy," is one who shares in the divine life of Christ. The New Testament refers to the "poor saints in Jerusalem" and in Acts, Luke refers to Peter visiting the "saints in Lydda," one of whom he cured from paralysis (Acts 9:32).

Saints are the sort of people who are never satisfied with a "doing what we've always done" approach to life. There is never the slightest chance of them falling into a rut, because saints are men and women who want to do what Jesus wants. And that can lead to a very exciting life. "They are led," wrote Father John Dalrymple, "into mad escapades of folly and scandal like Franz Jägerstätter refusing to serve in the German Army when everyone else did or, like Charles de Foucauld, going off to live with the Saharan Tuaregs as one of them."

Now this tendency to approach life in completely novel and fresh ways makes it very difficult to say exactly what a saint is. There is no ready-made mold into which we can pour the required virtues needed to make a saint.

We sometimes think we have the gift of recognizing true sanctity but if it were possible to choose any saint from the Church's calendar and invite him or her to dinner, we would probably get quite a shock. Plaster statues of very calm and quiet-looking saints serve to remind us that the saints are always ready to help and keep their memory before us. But they rarely capture the energy and enthusiasm of men and women who are always ready to turn the world on its head.

The truth, of course, is that many biographies of the saints down the years have made them out to be solemn-faced fanatics. Good fanatics, holy fanatics, but fanatics none the less. And that's a great pity, for it has left us with a stereotype image of the saint that not many of us would like to imitate. After all, who wants to be a fanatic?

To understand the true greatness of the saint, we have always to remember that saints are men and women of flesh and blood. The canonized saints were people with limitations just like the rest of us. They were people who allowed God's grace to work in them and, even after they had attained great holiness, kept their own distinctive personalities. First and foremost a saint is a human being. What makes the saint different from the rest of us is a complete openness to the promptings of the Spirit.

There is a saint and a sinner in us all. But if we do choose to be a saint, to follow the promptings of the Spirit, we will be an entirely unique kind of saint. For as Evelyn Waugh once wrote, "There is only one saint that Bridget Hogan can actually become, Saint Bridget Hogan. She cannot slip into heaven in fancy dress, made up as Saint Joan of Arc."

New life

Death is a rebirth. Our first birth is that moment when, as a baby, we break out from the womb into a new world. As a baby within the security of the womb, we cannot contemplate what the world outside is like. Birth is a shocking experience yet it is necessary for life and for growth beyond imagination. In our present world—the womb in which we now live—we cannot speak intelligently of what awaits us. The Scriptures speak of death as a new birth when we break out of the womb and enter a new creation. The next world into which we are born is the kingdom of God beyond our imagining.

"I think that what we suffer in this life can never be compared to the glory, as yet unrevealed, which is waiting for us....From the beginning till now the entire creation, as we know, has been groaning in one great act of giving birth; and not only creation, but all of us who possess the first-fruits of the Spirit, we too groan inwardly as we wait for our bodies to be set free" (Romans 8:18-23).

17. "The Holy Spirit will come upon you"

Mary in the Church

When it comes to talents, some people are loaded: they are bright, artistic, personable, good-looking, sought after—as well as not having a big head. Some people strive hard for talents that others seem to possess effortlessly. There are people who train, sweat, struggle, diet, try and say the right things, try to please, smile endlessly and yet—for all their efforts—they seem to be overlooked.

This is somewhat like the rich prince in the fairy tale who goes into serious training and tries every charm in the book to win the heart of the princess. And then she goes off regardless to marry a penniless woodcutter who didn't do anything spectacular to win her favor. The woodcutter is chosen because of the mysterious preference of the princess's love. And the prince is left wondering why he couldn't earn the love of the princess.

Like our friend the prince, when we see how some people are chosen, we sometimes ask: "What did they do to deserve that?" We presume that they did something special and we get tangled up trying to scrutinize their performance. And in all this we forget the freedom of the one who chose them in the first place.

The life of Mary, the mother of Jesus, reminds us of the extravagance of the love of God who freely chose Mary and whose choice made her "full of grace." Quite simply, Mary was loaded with gifts from the beginning of her life. There's no point in asking what Mary did to deserve that; she didn't do anything to deserve it because it was sheer gift. Nobody deserves gifts. Gifts reflect the generosity of the giver, not the worthiness of the receiver.

The greatest gift that Mary was given was to be chosen to be the mother of the Son of God. He began his life as a human being at the words of the angel Gabriel: "The Holy Spirit will come upon you." This was the turning point of history. Mary was asked by the Father to become the mother of the Lord and, by the power of the Holy Spirit, the Son of God was conceived as a human being and born into our world with the name of Jesus.

This choice by God is not the reward for dedicated work on the part of Mary; it is the result of God's freedom to choose Mary in a special way. Yet when God chooses Mary, that choice makes her worthy—a truth reflected in the *Magnificat* when Mary prays:

> **My soul glorifies the Lord and my spirit**
> **rejoices in God my savior;**
> **because he has looked on the lowliness**
> **of his handmaid.**
> **Yes, from this day forward,**
> **all generations will call me blessed,**
> **for the Almighty has done great things for me.**

Because of God's preference, because he has looked on Mary in a special way, all generations—as we do today—call her blessed. For Mary's talents were put to work for a mission that was not for herself; her mission in God's plan was to give Jesus to every generation of the human family.

Some people think that because Mary was so talented she is no longer human. Certainly, Mary has a unique role: as the Church teaches, she "occupies a place in the Church which is the highest after Christ and closest to us" (*Lumen Gentium* 54). Being chosen does not exclude her from the human race or free her from her choice. Mary still has to put her freedom at the service of God's plan.

The difference between us and Mary is not that Mary is chosen and we are not: it is that she fully responded to being chosen for her role, while we remain half-hearted about responding to ours. As Saint Paul once reminded us, we are all chosen: "He chose us, chose us in Christ, to be holy and spotless and to live through love in his presence" (Ephesians 1:4).

Like Mary, we face God's choice of us; like her we are challenged to say yes. If we could see ourselves as a result of God's choice—rather than a random mistake—we might be eager to say yes. God chose every single one of us and he has a role for each of us. He waits for our choice to put our freedom at his service.

Mary, Mother of God

The title "Mother of God," which is given to Mary, can cause some confusion. There is only one way to become a member of the human race and that is to be born of a woman. God who created us wanted to be right at the heart of his creation and so he wanted to become human too. God became man in the person of Jesus Christ, and Mary was his mother.

In Jesus Christ, God became man. Jesus Christ is truly God and truly human. He is the one mediator between God and ourselves. He brings heaven to earth and men and women to God. Mary, as the human mother of Jesus Christ, can be called the "God-bearer."

During the first five centuries of the Church, there were many theories going around about how Jesus Christ was both God and man. Some emphasized his divinity, others were more concerned with his humanity. Finally, the Council of Ephesus in 431 resolved the argument by declaring Jesus Christ as being truly God and truly man. Consequently, the Council also stated that Mary was not only the mother of Christ, but also the Mother of God. If we say that Mary is not the Mother of God, then Jesus Christ is not God and we are not saved. The title is, in fact, saying more about Jesus Christ than about Mary.

Mary, then, is truly the Mother of God if two conditions are fulfilled; that she is really the mother of Jesus and that Jesus is really God.

A pattern for every Christian

In recognizing herself as being chosen by God, Mary sets the pattern for every Christian. She is filled with the Holy Spirit of God; she is graceful. Pope Paul VI, in his apostolic exhortation *Marialis Cultus*, summarizes this pattern. He emphasizes four aspects of her life which clearly illustrate how "the Almighty has done great things for her" and how we, too, may discover that God has done great things for us and has chosen each one of us.

■ Mary is the attentive Virgin. In order to live according to the word of God we must first be prepared to listen to it. This means attending to the word of God in the Scriptures and in the circumstances of our lives even when we don't understand what is happening to us. For Mary herself did not understand the message of God that she would become the mother of the Lord when she asked, "How can this come about for I am a virgin?" This attentiveness includes the wisdom to look back on the events of our life, just as Mary "stored up in her heart" the events of the birth of Jesus and his life in Nazareth and so grew in faith.

■ Mary is the Virgin in prayer. From the moment she was chosen to be the mother of Jesus and praised God in the words of the *Magnificat* to the moment after Jesus' ascension when Mary is described in the Acts of the Apostles as "joined in continuous prayer" with the other disciples, she is praying—approaching God for those in need. She continues this prayer today. Such prayer, the result of familiarity and a comfort with God, is the principal task of every follower of Jesus, for it brings about the ever-growing closeness between God and his people.

■ Mary is the Virgin-Mother. This was a miraculous motherhood, a sign that the Father of Jesus was not a human being (Mary's husband, Joseph, is known as Jesus' foster-father) but God himself. The fruitfulness of her life is a sign of the whole Church which, in the sacrament of baptism, "brings forth to a new and immortal life children who are conceived by the power of the Holy Spirit and born of God." And it is a sign, too, of the source of our own fruitfulness, because our true success and happiness in life doesn't depend on our own gifts and graces but on the power of God and the gift of the Holy Spirit who comes to help us in our weakness.

■ Mary is the Virgin presenting offerings. The work of Mary reached its climax on Calvary where Christ offered himself as the perfect sacrifice to God and where Mary stood by the cross suffering grievously with her only Son. Mary, then, is above all the example of that worship that consists in making one's life an offering to God. This offering of one's life in faith is the central core of the Christian life. Just as Jesus offered himself, and Mary with him, we are chosen to give our lives to the Father. In human terms this is impossible to understand for it is always accompanied by weakness and suffering. But Mary's "yes" is for all of us the path to new life since it shows us the way to true happiness and fulfillment in the kingdom of God.

Now you too, in him, have heard the message of the truth and the good news of your salvation, and have believed it; and you too have been stamped with the seal of the Holy Spirit of the Promise, the pledge of our inheritance which brings freedom for those whom God has taken for his own, to make his glory praised.

Ephesians 1:13-14

18. Appendix

Using This Book in the RCIA

Your Faith is a thumbnail sketch of what we believe as Catholic Christians. By no means a compendium of doctrine, it follows a logical path of conversion and life in the Spirit, using as its touchstone the articles of faith that are professed in the Nicene Creed—our belief in

- God the Father
- God's Son, Jesus, born of a virgin, tortured and put to death, and risen from the dead
- God's Holy Spirit, giver and sustainer of all life
- the communion of saints which is the Church
- the forgiveness of sins
- bodily resurrection and everlasting life

As such, it is an ideal vehicle for use within an RCIA program. And because the index is cross referenced to the *Catechism of the Catholic Church*, this book can be the means for engaging in a more in-depth study of the history, tradition, and dogma of the Catholic Church. Or you may supplement it with materials such as Liguori's *Journey of Faith*. Regardless of your methodology, be sure to begin with a copy of the Nicene Creed. The Creed is our faith; it is what

we believe. All other "articles of faith" are secondary to these bedrock truths.

As you move through the contents of *Your Faith*, be sure you can identify where each section "fits" in the Nicene Creed. This book is a "profession of faith." Also, go to the "Questions for Discussion and Reflection" below and on page 94 and reflect on the questions posed there for each section of this book. Keep a notebook handy and journal your reflections as you go along. End each study session with prayer. Pray in whatever way(s) you are most comfortable engaging God in communication. If you feel "dry" and prayer-less, or think that you don't yet know how to pray, journal on those thoughts and feelings. You will soon find that your journal will become both a prayer book and a tool for future discoveries of yourself and *your faith*.

Finally, *Your Faith* is designed to whet your appetite for more: more knowledge and a deepening spirituality. Check out the additional resources listed on page 95. And welcome to the mysterious and wonderful community that we call Church. May you abide with us and render us a better and more complete Church than we are without you.

Questions for Discussion and Reflection

Chapter 1: The Spirit of Life
What makes life worth living for you? How do you accept and handle change? Describe a time when life especially made sense to you. Describe a time when life felt confusing and senseless.

Chapter 2: The Rumor of the Spirit of God
What is your image of God? Has it changed over time? How has your faith in God helped you in your life? How do you experience God's presence in your life? How do you experience God's absence? Do you think that the Ten Commandments are relevant in today's culture? If you were to decide to read the Old Testament, with which book would you chose to begin your reading?

Chapter 3: The Spirit of the Lord Has Been Given to Me
Thinking back, describe who the person of Jesus has been to you. How do the words "prophet without honor in his own land" apply to John the Baptist? Do you feel that God has invited you to love him? What is God asking of you today?

Chapter 4: My Words Are Spirit and They Are Life
What does Jesus as "the Way, the Truth, and the Life" mean to you? What makes Jesus special to you? How might you have responded if you had been "called" to be one of Jesus' disciples? Do you consider yourself a disciple of Jesus now? If so, in what way? How does the fact of Christ's Resurrection affect you? Think of and describe any of God's miracles of love or power that are in evidence today.

Chapter 5: The Spirit Will Teach You Everything

What is the place of Scripture in your current life? Name some people in the New Testament who are important to you. Why? God commands us to love one another; how do you express this in terms of your own life? Of the four gospels, which one is most significant to you. Why? Do you see the Holy Spirit alive in your world today? If so, how?

Chapter 6: The Spirit for Our Wounded World

Why is there so much suffering in the world? What part do I believe that God plays in it? Each person has his or her own form of "darkness." What "darkness" do you exhibit to which Jesus could bring some light and healing? Do you see any benefits in having faith? At what point in your life did you first experience faith in the Word of God? What people of faith do you know and imitate? The Apostles' Creed and the Nicene Creed are expressions of Catholic beliefs. Find copies of these creeds and choose those tenets that you most relate to.

Chapter 7: The Spirit of God Has Made a Home in You

What masks do you wear for others? How do you hide from yourself? From God? What kind of prayer do you do personally? How does your prayer style differ from others? Which elements of the Our Father are most significant to you? What fears, hopes, and sorrows do you bring to God in prayer?

Chapter 8: Always the Same Spirit

What evidence can you gather to show that the Church is a community? The Church has a visible structure: what experiences did you have with the Church as an institutional structure? How do you see the Church promoting peace, justice, and social concerns? What is the effect on the Church when some of its members sin grievously and publicly? What is your definition of Church? How can the Church be compared to the Holy Trinity?

Chapter 9: The Creative Spirit

How does (or will) baptism make you "different"? What does it mean to "die with Christ"? What does the process of "journeying" to Catholicism mean to you? Why is water an appropriate sign to use in the sacrament of baptism? What is the meaning of the lighted candle and the white garment in the baptismal rite? How do these symbols help to underscore the meaning of the sacrament of baptism?

Chapter 10: The Living Spirit

Are you ready to affirm and be confirmed in the faith of the Catholic Church? Why or why not? Candidates for confirmation are anointed with the Oil of Chrism: What meaning does this have for you? How do you accept your own failings and the failings of others?

Chapter 11: The Nurturing Spirit

How does the Word of God feed you in the Mass? Why is being present for the Eucharist important to you? Why do you think that one name for the Eucharist is Holy Communion? What evidence do you see that the gifts of the Holy Spirit exist in your life? What is your definition of the Eucharist?

Chapter 12: The Trusting Spirit

Ask priests who you know about the meaning of their vocations. Share your information with others. How is the Church organized? Discuss the relationships among each level of the Church's hierarchy?

Chapter 13: The Sharing Spirit

How does the Church's vision of the sacrament of marriage affect you personally? How well is the Church's vision of marriage accepted by our culture at large? What benefits are created by the sacrament of marriage?

Chapter 14: The Healing Spirit

How do you face up to sin in your life? What are you willing to do to heal the sins of the world? When have you experienced true forgiveness? What value do you see in telling your sins to another person? Is sin a reality to you?

Chapter 15: The Saving Spirit

What can you do to comfort and help heal those who are suffering? Have you ever been anointed? What is your belief about life after death? How has your faith helped you at the time of someone's death who was close to you? In what way do you see death as joyful?

Chapter 16: Reborn in the Spirit

How have you experienced the communion of saints? What is your vision of purgatory? How do you imagine the Last Judgment?

Chapter 17: The Holy Spirit Will Come Upon You

What is your experience with Mary? How do you respond to her immaculate conception? Her perpetual virginity? Would you have stood at the foot of the cross and watched Jesus die? Do you pray the rosary and the Hail Mary?

Additional Resources

Being Catholic Today: Your Personal Guide: With Questions for Reflection or Discussion and Action Ideas by Bert Ghezzi. Servant Publications, 1998. 160 pages, paperback, ISBN: 1569550107. $9.99.

Believing Catholic (Faith Essentials) by Archbishop Daniel E. Pilarczyk. St. Anthony Messenger Press, 1999. 82 pages, paperback, ISBN: 0867163860. $6.95

Believing in Jesus: A Popular Overview of the Catholic Faith by Leonard Foley, O.F.M., and Jeremy Harrington, O.F.M. St. Anthony Messenger Press, 2001. 240 pages, paperback, ISBN: 0867164123. $9.95.

Catholic Beliefs From A to Z by Alfred McBride, O.Praem. Servant Publications, 2001. 189 pages, paperback, ISBN: 156955174X. #12.99.

Catholic Source Book by Rev. Peter Klein. Harcourt, 1999. 512 pages, paperback, ISBN: 015956530. $20.95.

The Catechism Handbook by Oscar Lukefahr, C.M. Liguori Publications, 128 pages, paperback, ISBN: 0-89243-864-9. $12.95.

A Catholic Guide to the Bible (Revised and Expanded) by Oscar Lukefahr, C.M. Liguori Publications, 224 pages, paperback, ISBN: 0-7648-0201-1. $7.95.

The Catholic Virtues: Seven Pillars of a Good Life by Mitch Finley. Liguori Publications, 144 pages, paperback, ISBN: 0-7648-0487-1. $12.95.

The Essential Catholic Handbook: A Summary of Beliefs, Practices, and Prayers, Redemptorist Pastoral Publication. Liguori Publications, 304 pages, paperback, ISBN: 0-89243-910-6. $9.95.

The Essential Catholic Handbook of the Sacraments: A Summary of Beliefs, Rites, and Prayers, With a Glossary of Key Terms, Redemptorist Pastoral Publication. Liguori Publications, 304 pages, paperback, ISBN: 0-7648-0781-1. $13.95.

The Essential Mary Handbook: A Summary of Beliefs, Devotions, and Prayers, Redemptorist Pastoral Publication. Liguori Publications, 304 pages, paperback, ISBN: 0-7648-0383-2. $13.95.

Exploring the Catholic Church: An Introduction to Catholic Teaching and Practice by Marcellino D'Amborio, Ph.D. Charis Books, 2001. 170 pages, paperback, ISBN: 1569553017. $9.99.

Following Christ: How to Live a Moral Life by Daniel Lowery. Liguori Publications, 192 pages, paperback, ISBN: 0-89243-850-9. $12.95.

Handbook for Today's Catholic. Fully Indexed to the Catechism of the Catholic Church, Redemptorist Pastoral Publication. Liguori Publications, 112 pages, booklet, ISBN: 0-89243-671-9. $2.95.

The Privilege of Being Catholic by Oscar Lukefahr, C.M. Liguori Publications, 208 pages, paperback, ISBN: 0-89243-563-1. $7.95.

The Seven Gifts of the Holy Spirit by Mitch Finley. Liguori Publications, 144 pages, paperback, ISBN: 0-7648-0719-6. $12.95.

The Ten Commandments: Timeless Challenges for Today by Mitch Finley. Liguori Publications, 144 pages, paperback, ISBN: 0-7648-0663-7. $12.95.

We Believe: A Survey of the Catholic Faith (Revised and Cross-Referenced to the Catechism of the Catholic Church) by Oscar Lukefahr, C.M. Liguori Publications, 224 pages, paperback, ISBN: 0-89243-536-4. $7.95.

Would You Like to Be a Catholic? by Eugene Kennedy. St. Anthony Messenger Press, 2003. 96 pages, paperback, ISBN: 0867165308. $8.95.

Why Catholic?: Catholic Answers to Our Protestant Brothers and Sisters in Christ by John J. Pasquini. St. Bedes Publications, 2001. 132 pages, paperback, ISBN: 1879007452. $18.00.

Index and Correlations to
CATECHISM OF THE CATHOLIC CHURCH